Parliamentary Papers of John Robinson, 1774-1784;

William Thomas Laprade

BIBLIOLIFE

PARLIAMENTARY PAPERS
OF JOHN ROBINSON
1774-1784

EDITED FOR THE ROYAL HISTORICAL SOCIETY

BY

WILLIAM THOMAS LAPRADE, Ph.D.

Professor of History in Trinity College, North Carolina

LONDON
OFFICES OF THE SOCIETY
22 RUSSELL SQUARE, W.C.1.
1922

INTRODUCTION

O F John Robinson personally we need say little here, for his personality was merged in the office that he held for more than a decade. He was born and baptized at St. Lawrence, Appleby, Westmorland, August 14, 1727, the eldest son of Charles Robinson, a prosperous tradesman of that town, and was trained in the law. He inherited a comfortable fortune and was brought into parliament for Appleby by Sir James Lowther in 1764. He served for that constituency until his break with Sir James, when he found a safe seat at Harwich, which he represented until his death, becoming in the end himself the patron of that borough. There is ample evidence that Robinson was happy in his marriage to Mary Crowe, daughter of a West India merchant and planter, and that he was devoted to his daughter Mary, whose marriage to Henry Nevill, later second Earl of Abergavenny, gave him much satisfaction.

Robinson had a wide acquaintance among men active in the affairs of his time both in business and in politics. He was an intimate of Charles Jenkinson, the leader of the King's Friends after the retirement of Bute and later first Earl of Liverpool; also of Richard Atkinson who accumulated a fortune in the course of the American war from his contracts, particularly from that to furnish rum to the troops in America. He hunted with Richard Rigby, who was Paymaster of the Forces in the period of the American war, when it was a profitable office to hold. Warren Hastings corresponded with him regularly and had from him knowledge of the policies of North's administration, frequently in advance of the time when the information could be obtained from the minister himself. Having a large measure of the scriptural quality of diligence in business, Robinson became the trusted counsellor of the king, and George III had few servants whom he trusted so implicitly or who pleased him so well.

v

Of the office that Robinson held in the period of the dates of most of the papers in this volume more needs to be said. In fact, a whole book might be written on the history of this office and the holders thereof which would more illumine the dynamic forces in the government of the kingdom than have books written about other offices of greater distinction. " The officers of the Treasury Board," says a document prepared about the time Robinson was quitting his office, " are two secretaries, four chief clerks, an indefinite number of other clerks, together with messengers and other servants. The business of the two secretaries hath been usually divided as follows : The elder secretary receives all papers that are to be brought before the Board ; when the Board sits he presents them for consideration, stating the purport of them, signs all letters for the issuing of money, peruses warrants prepared for the King's signature, and superintends all parliamentary business."[1]

It was the duty of the junior secretary to keep the minutes of the board and to attend to other proper secretarial business. Aside from the responsible task of signing all " letters for issuing money," Robinson, who was the senior secretary, was primarily engaged in the superintendence of parliamentary business. The term " elder " had, of course, no reference to seniority of appointment. Grey Cooper, who was Robinson's secretarial colleague, had served in the junior office for five years before Robinson was appointed to the senior position.

The parliamentary business referred to, of which most of the papers in this volume are relics, was largely analogous to the work of the present " Whip." It was the business of the senior secretary to see that a comfortable majority of the supporters of the administration were present in the lobby when divisions were necessary and to manage the constituencies so that a favourable majority would be returned in the case of elections. Most of the papers here printed have to do with the latter duty. Robinson, while in office, had the superintendence of two general elections, in 1774 and in 1780. The election of 1784 was practically conducted under his supervision since George Rose, then Senior Secretary to the

---

[1] *Chatham Papers*, Public Record Office, 231. This description of the working of the Treasury and the allied departments of the British government was prepared in the year between June, 1782, and June, 1783, no doubt in the administration of Shelburne when Pitt was Chancellor of the Exchequer.

Treasury, was a novice in the office, having been appointed only a few months before.

For fifteen years, therefore, Robinson had a unique opportunity to observe the factors potent in the action of the British parliament. No other man in his time, and few in any other time, had the privilege of watching from so intimate a point of vantage the ebb and flow of party support. Several factors contribute to give these fifteen years a peculiar interest. George III was still busy in his efforts to regain somewhat of the share in the government lost to the Crown in the reigns of his immediate predecessors. He took an active personal part in the election of 1780, supplying plentifully both advice and funds. Robinson was his chief and most trusted lieutenant in this enterprise and afterwards the agent for negotiating the payment of the deficit that such an undertaking usually leaves in its wake. We are not surprised, therefore, to find among these papers items of information supplementing knowledge long public on these points. The papers relating to this election, however, and those relating to the election of 1774 do little more than fill in the details of the picture ; they make no important change in the outline.

In the six years between 1774 and 1780 Robinson acquired skill in the duties and methods of his office. The facts that had seemed to be of primary importance when he was making ready for his first general election, he had by the end of that period absorbed as a part of his working knowledge as far as he had need of them at all. By 1780 he would probably have regarded it as the work of an amateur to list the offices " tenable with seats in Lords and Commons " or the members of the national legislature holding such offices. He would most certainly have placed a lower estimate on the importance of the Lord Lieutenant, as such, as a factor in county elections. He had learned the real sources of power, and he knew whom to approach. When Shelburne requested him in the summer of 1782 to furnish " an accurate state of the House of Commons and the connections of each of them as far as can be ascertained,"[1] he could speak with a large degree of authority. Unfortunately only a fragment of this statement is preserved in this collection of papers ; in the entire document we would have an intimate picture of an eighteenth-century House of Commons such as now exists nowhere in print.

[1] Page 42.

Nobody appreciated better than Robinson the difficulties added to his task in preparing this statement by the events that had transpired since the general election in 1780. The House of Commons then chosen, though typical in membership of the parliaments of the time, supported in the course of its life of less than four years almost every existing shade of party opinion. It was elected, as the papers in this volume afford additional evidence, at a considerable personal outlay by George III, to support the measures of that monarch and his minister, and it played that rôle loyally until the surrender of Cornwallis afforded to North the escape from office he had so long sought. After North's resignation the combination of Rockingham Whigs and Chathamites commanded a majority in the same House of Commons until the death of the Whig leader completed the dissolution of that coalition and threw the government into the hands of the Chathamites in alliance with the supporters of the king. The combination of the Whigs with North and the personal following he had acquired while in office procured the support of an ample majority in the House of Commons for the ministry the king reluctantly appointed from this group, and the same House of Commons, before its dissolution in 1784, finally voted in support of the adminstration led by the youthful William Pitt. Nevertheless, the contemporary pamphleteer described accurately other parliaments of the period when he said of this one : " The last parliament and the present parliament are very nearly one and the same It is true indeed there have been some exchanges, and different branches of particular families have taken their rotations in election honours ; but still both parliaments are essentially and effectually alike " [1]

Little wonder Robinson found trouble in making a report on such a parliament to a minister who cherished " measures " more than " men " Measures or questions of public policy were rarely primary motives in the choice of members in an eighteenth-century House of Commons, and Robinson did not in his statement take cognizance of a possible difference of opinion on the peace with France and America recently negotiated, or any other similar issue He came instead immediately to the practical point. " Nothing," he said, " can be more difficult than to form a state of the political sentiments of the House of Commons in the present juncture. In

[1] *Commonplace Arguments against Administration with Obvious Answers*, p. 12.

a stable, permanent government to whom gentlemen have professed
friendship, with whom they have in general acted, and from whom
they have received favours, conjectures may be formed with a
tolerable certainty of the opinions 'which gentlemen will entertain
on particular questions, but in a state so rent as this has lately been,
torn by intestinal divisions, and split into different parties, with
an administration to be established after one has been overturned
and another divided, it is the hardest task that can be to class
them." He concluded his prefatory statement with the admonition
that the conclusions submitted " must be subject to much discussion
and explanation on every part of it to comprehend the minute and
true state of each part and of individuals."[1]

The key to success in almost every parliamentary constituency
in Robinson's time was in some individual or comparatively small
group of individuals. This was as true in cases where there were
a considerable number of voters as where the franchise was less
widely distributed. Appeals, to be effective, had to be made to
these sources of power   Not public opinion or popular feeling, but
" interest " and " influence " were the terms most in use by a
practical electioneerer.

Writers since 1832 have found it difficult to apprehend the character of the parliaments in the last decades of the eighteenth century.
There has been a tendency to pronounce them unrepresentative
and hopelessly corrupt on the one hand or to assume on the other
that by some occult process the British people gave expression to
popular feeling in an election in which most of them had no share.
The truth is, the parliaments just previous to 1832, like those in
the next succeeding generation, and in fact like those of to-day, were
representative of the ruling group of the time. The ruling class
was simply in the process of being enlarged; it was much smaller
in the middle of the eighteenth century than in 1832, infinitely
smaller than it is to-day. The people, in the number that participate
in the elections to-day, could not express their will even to an
approximate degree with the machinery of election in vogue in
Robinson's time. There are many reasons for assuming, however,
that the comparatively small group of persons who had a share
in the government of Great Britain then was able to make its
wishes prevail. In other words, the ruling class in Robinson's day
was actually represented in the House of Commons of the period.

[1] Page 42.

The difference is that, to-day, we ascertain the popular will by means of an election; in the eighteenth century an election seldom gave evidence of the views of the ruling class one way or the other. Parliamentary seats were simply the perquisites of the members of the ruling group, whether they occupied them personally or others sat on their nomination. It made little difference whether the members of the ruling group held burgages or had the trouble and expense of a " potwalloper " election. In the few constituencies in which opinion might have been voiced by the people *en masse* contested elections were dreaded as an evil and were seldom held if it was possible to avoid them.

The impression has somehow crept into many of the books that the freeholders in the counties were responsive to the agitation of public questions and made their wishes prevail in the choice of members of the House of Commons in a larger degree than did the voters in the boroughs. Apropos of this view a pamphleteer of Robinson's time suggested to a contemporary who upheld it that he " desire Mr. Byng or Mr. Robinson to inform him how many county members are now in this parliament [1780] or were in the last who are not the entire nominations of peers. He will find one half of them, at least, are the near relatives or connections of peers, without property or pretence except such relationship or connection to be chosen by a county; almost another fourth are elected by some two or three peers; and I believe that it will be allowed to me that if the peers in every county were to unite they could nominate every county member except one."[1] An examination of the papers of Robinson published in this volume tends to confirm this statement. In consequence of this condition contested elections in the counties were even less frequent than in other constituencies. According to information collected by Henry Stooks Smith,[2] in the seven general elections held in the period from the accession of George III to the end of the century, in which the fifty-two counties of England and Wales chose in the aggregate 644 members of the House of Commons, there were in all only fifty-seven unsuccessful candidacies in these constituencies. That is, fewer than one in eleven of the members who sat for the counties of England and Wales in these years met with even nominal opposition.

[1] *A Letter to Mr. Debrett, being an Answer to Lucubrations during a short Recess*, p. 23.
[2] *Parliaments of England*, three volumes, published in London, 1844–50.

In Yorkshire, a county noted for the number and independence of its freeholders, a local politician wrote in a private letter in 1782 .

In this county the public sense on political questions can scarcely be taken pure and unmixed with the influence of provincial parties , therefore our discussions are not so important as you are pleased to consider them, or, as from the population and real consequence of the county they ought to be. Two great interests, opposed from generation to generation, have almost equally divided the county into opposite factions . . . *Great active exertion* it is difficult to obtain from even one party on any proposition that does not contain in it a provincial interest. Our zeal exhausts itself in the county cause and leaves us cold to mere public questions [1]

There was not in Yorkshire a single contested election in the period from 1760 to 1800.

The conclusion from all of this and from the information contained in Robinson's papers is not that the people and parliaments of the last decades of the eighteenth century were corrupt beyond those of subsequent times   There were merely different instrumentalities. for exercising political power, totally unsuited to later conditions, not perhaps to be commended for any time, but accepted as a matter of course by most of the patriotic Britons who participated by their use in the task of governing the kingdom

More than one student has been led astray on this subject by the circumstances of the last general election in which Robinson was an active participant. Fortunately we have in this collection of papers more detailed evidence of the methods used in that election than we have in the case of the two previous elections that Robinson supervised in his official capacity. This election involved other factors in addition to those previously wont to participate effectively in parliamentary elections. In the degree that these new forces determined the result, there is an element of fact in the general assumption that the unpopularity of Fox and North is seen in the result of the election in 1784   But we should bear in mind that these new claimants for admission into the favoured class of the ruling group adopted the only method open to them for making their wishes prevail.

I have undertaken to show elsewhere the degree to which public opinion, as we understand that term, was influential in determining.

[1] Christopher Wyvill, *Political Papers*, IV. 242.

the result in the general election of 1784, citing the papers here published as part of the evidence.[1] Had not the minister whose lease of power was confirmed by the results of that election continued in office through an heroic time, and had not some of his personal followers survived into a period when a stigma attaches to certain practices prevalent in the eighteenth century not generally felt in 1784, it is doubtful whether the legend that Great Britain witnessed in that year a popular rally to support a leader of reform could ever have been taken seriously. Inasmuch as this legend has reached a proportion that induces Pitt's most substantial biographer in recent years to proclaim him the " champion of purity in elections "[2] it is fortunate that Robinson preserved in such detail the material for telling the story of the election of that parliament. This is all the more fortunate in that the habit of assuming the fact of this premature assertion of a popular voice in the government has tended to obscure an understanding of the forces that promoted the growth of popular government when it actually came to exist.

As has been pointed out before,[3] Pitt declined the urgent solicitation of George III in March, 1783, that he should form an administration, largely on the ground that there was no immediate prospect that he could command the support of a majority of the members of the House of Commons. Being unable to secure a leader for what appeared to be a forlorn hope, the king unwillingly appointed Fox and North to office, confessing thereby the impotence of the combined strength of the Chathamites and his own personal following as against the " Coalition." The ministry thus formed, though not in favour with the king, had the support of a majority of the ruling class as then constituted, and particularly of the members of the House of Commons, until the agitation on the East India question.

Neither the authorship nor the merits of Fox's famous Bill need detain us here. There is no doubt that it stimulated in most of those who had a stake in the affairs of the Company a fear that their interests were endangered. Moreover, there were newcomers in the Company who had accumulated their wealth in part at least in the course of the American war, of whom Richard Atkinson was leader and a type, who shared these fears. The supporters of the king and the Chathamites were thus reinforced in their opposition

[1] *English Historical Review*, XXXI. 224.
[2] J. Holland Rose, *William Pitt and National Revival*, p. 272.
[3] *American Historical Review*, XVIII. 254.

to the coalition by these commercial magnates unified for the time
being by what seemed to be a danger to their common interests.
As the Bill made its progress through the House of Commons the
Company proprietors became the more frantic in their determination
to prevent at any cost its ultimate passage into law. Atkinson
came forward as a leader to co-operate with Jenkinson. On the
same day that the Bill finally passed the lower house by the over-
whelming vote of 208 to 102 he wrote to Robinson : " Everything
stands prepared for the blow if a certain person has courage to strike
it." He wrote again the same day repeating the suggestion, made
at a meeting he had just attended, that the proprietors would better
surrender their " violated rights to the Crown in a solemn way if
the bill passes the House of Peers than let these new potentates
have the power to mismanage our property without controul." [1]

No evidence is available to identify the man who suggested the
scheme ultimately adopted. Jenkinson and Atkinson seem to
have been the prime movers in agitating the matter, but they did
not lack support. Naturally these leaders confided in Robinson,
though the latter was careful not to be seen in town until his presence
was necessary. By December 12 Atkinson was in a position to
write that " a direct communication " had been had with the king
with the result that his majesty had given to Lord Temple, as is
well known, authority " to say (when it shall be necessary) that
whoever votes in the House of Lords for the India Bill is not his
friend," though this permission was to be kept secret for several
days.[2] Robinson's old friend Rigby, however, who was loyal to
North, his former chief, wrote on the same day, sanguine that the
bill would pass the upper house with a score of votes to spare.[3]

Meanwhile, in case of the successful accomplishment of the project
of defeating the bill in the House of Lords and having the king
dismiss his ministers in consequence, it was necessary to convince
Pitt that it was a feasible matter to procure the support of a majority
in the House of Commons. The task of adducing evidence for this
purpose was left to Robinson. The result is the most illuminating
description of an eighteenth-century House of Commons that has
yet come to light.[4] Not a constituency was neglected, and the
information was set down by the man in his generation best qualified
to speak with authority. He lays bare the identity of the hands

---

[1] *Historical Manuscripts Commission, Tenth Report,* Appendix, Pt. VI. p. 61.
   [2] Ibid., p. 62.   [3] Ibid., p. 62.   [4] Page 66.

that actually held the reins of power in Great Britain. The mistakes he made are easy to understand in view of the circumstances under which he prepared the paper, and they but confirm the essential correctness of the picture he drew.

By December 15 the projectors of the enterprise were ready to submit to Pitt conclusive evidence that it was a feasible undertaking with few risks to endanger its success. Accordingly, a meeting was appointed at the house of Dundas where, besides the host, Pitt, Robinson, and Atkinson met for the first of the conferences that Robinson had with the young statesman.[1] Within the space of three days thereafter the bill had been rejected by the Lords, and the king had dismissed his ministers and had appointed Pitt to lead a new administration.

Robinson had undertaken to estimate in advance the support that such an administration could hope to have both in the House of Commons chosen at the general election in 1780 and in another to be chosen in an election to be held after the new ministry should be organized. It was assumed at this time that the dissolution would not be delayed long after the change, because Robinson's estimates, which proved to have a substantial basis, did not promise support for the new administration until after the dissolution. He estimated that in the old parliament Pitt could count on the support of 149 certainly *pro* and 104 hopeful, while the coalition would have 231 certain and 74 doubtful, that is, hopeful from the coalition point of view. After the dissolution and a new election the tables would be turned. Pitt would have 253 *pro* with 116 hopeful, while the opposition would have only 123 certainly, with 66 doubtful. These estimates were made by Robinson in the seclusion of Syon Hill, and not once in his paper does he refer to the supposed unpopularity of the coalition or to the excited state of the public mind anent the India Bill. He dealt only in personalities and in methods of manipulation familiar to him from past experience.

He estimated that the county members would maintain substantially their first alignment, a natural forecast, since these constituencies were in control of the nobility or gentry as family perquisites. The largest proportion of the change would naturally occur in the close boroughs, because in these constituencies seats were procurable by the means possessed by those who were sponsors for the enterprise. The case of Scotland was easy ; Henry Dundas

[1] Page 105.

was party to the undertaking, and in most constituencies in that country Dundas was in a position to say, as Robinson quoted him as saying of the sitting member for Edinburgh, " *pro,* or he will not come in." [1] The English and Welsh constituencies sometimes required a greater degree of " management " or " attention," to quote two of Robinson's favourite terms

Knowing that immediate action on Robinson's suggestions in these matters would be essential, Atkinson wrote to him at noon, December 18 : " I am clearly of opinion that after the debate of last night disguise will no longer disguise anything and is therefore absurd. I have therefore suggested the sending an ostensible signification of commands to give information and hope you will agree in opinion that the kind of communication which will now become hourly necessary cannot be carried on at ten miles distance, and that you will come to town to-night or to-morrow." Atkinson had on the preceding day been elected to the directorate of the East India Company, and of the procedure in that body he told Robinson in the same letter : " We are to have a committee and a general court to-morrow when we must lay our groundwork." [2]

Apparently Robinson acted on this suggestion and began immediately to busy himself making ready for the election that was inevitable. It was soon apparent that in the management of this election he was to serve in an unofficial capacity. He was left out with Jenkinson and Atkinson in making the appointments to office. Perhaps Robinson would not have wished to have again his old position, but Jenkinson seems to have been chagrined that the ministry that he had played so conspicuous a part in making possible found no immediate need for his services, and gave expression to his disappointment in a letter to Robinson on December 24. [3] Atkinson had enough to occupy his time in his activities in the affairs of the company and in making preparations for the election. Robinson's old office went to George Rose, and it now became Robinson's task to initiate Rose into the duties of the position.

While Rose never acquired Robinson's skill in the task, he displayed considerable ability in the management of the elections held in the course of Pitt's first administration. No small part of

[1] Page 10.
[2] *Historical Manuscripts Commission, Tenth Report,* Appendix, Part VI. p. 63.
[3] Ibid , p 64.

his success in the office was probably due to this preliminary training he had from Robinson. The correspondence between Robinson and Rose in the process of the general election of 1784, printed in this volume, throws interesting light on the character of this training and on the prevailing methods of conducting elections. It is one of the few occasions when an incoming Secretary to the Treasury had the advice and assistance of his predecessor who had managed the last preceding general election.

The preliminary plans for the election of 1784 appear to have been made in the early conferences held at the house of Dundas before Atkinson summoned Robinson to town openly, and evidence of the character of these plans is preserved in the interesting memoranda contained in this volume, on the back of which Robinson later inscribed the curious endorsement: " Parliamentary state of boroughs and situations, with remarks, preparatory to a new parliament in 178[3] on a change of administration and Mr. Pitt's coming in, sketched out at several meetings at Lord Advocate Dundas's in Leicester Square, and a wild wide calculate of the money wanted for seats, but which I always disapproved and thought very wrong." [1]

It has been previously suggested [2] that Robinson may have penned the last clause in the above notation in his later years, having professed meanwhile a new theory of political morals different from that which he was accustomed to practise in his more active days There is, however, another and perhaps preferable view which it may be worth while to state here since it involves the mooted point of the new dynamic in the general election of 1784 not manifest on so large a scale in former years.

There is no evidence to show that Robinson's conscience was ever troubled on account of the methods he used habitually in 1774 and in 1780 and in intervening by-elections, and he had been wont to arrange for the purchase of any marketable seats and for the customary corruption of venal boroughs. He had expended for George III the funds which that frugal monarch regularly and surreptitiously saved for election purposes from his privy purse, and he never hesitated to adopt any method of bargain or barter that seemed likely to procure a seat. However, neither Robinson nor his contemporaries who engaged in these practices seem to have felt that they were doing anything untoward or unworthy

[1] Page 106. [2] *English Historical Review*, XXXI. 231.

of a patriotic subject of the British crown. It was simply the prevailing method of procuring a seat in parliament or of promoting the choice of a majority to support a ministry, a method used by all parties and called in question only by a few radical agitators for reform A general election was simply an occasion for a readjustment of interests and a redistribution of favours. It would have seemed to most men who had a part in these tasks, much more to a broker like Robinson, as unjust to accuse them of corruption as it would have seemed unreasonable to assume that the business of governing the kingdom ought to rest in the untutored hands of the mass of its inhabitants. It is not easy for us to-day to appreciate the state of mind of public men in that time, but it is essential that we do it if we are to appraise the motives of their action.

Granting this point, what in the projected methods for the general election of 1784 was so radically different from the customary practice that it raised doubts in the mind of Robinson ? May it not have been the prospect that the commercial magnates, though his own friends, would use their wealth in large amounts in an organized and systematic way, not merely to purchase seats regularly in the market, to provide funds for the satisfaction of electors habitually venal, and to establish interests in the accustomed way, but also frankly in an effort to destroy, by the use of large sums, interests long established and to corrupt constituencies not hitherto regarded as venal ? That is, this new power of organized wealth, aroused to give battle in defence of its privileges, now proposed to depart from the accepted rules of the game and to adopt a policy of winning at any cost. The men active in the company felt that the existence of that organization and of the property and privileges held by its members were in danger ; they proposed to use every available weapon to guard themselves against this attack. Perhaps they saw little or no difference between the moral quality of the methods they proposed to adopt and those habitually used by Robinson and his predecessors in office.

But Robinson knew that there was a real and radical difference. He did not sympathize with the proposed methods, in the first place because, from his knowledge of conditions, he felt that they were unnecessary to compass the ends sought by his friends. He knew it was wellnigh impossible to return a House of Commons unfavourable to an administration possessed at the same time of the reins of power and the favour of the king. Therefore, he had

no fear that Pitt would find himself in a minority in the new parliament ; he had offered facts to substantiate this view. Having the
instincts of a sportsman, he felt, in the second place, perhaps without
being able to formulate his uneasiness in a definite way, that this
introduction of crude wealth as a stark force for the purpose of
overturning the established order in the constituencies would mark
the beginning of the end of the parliamentary régime with which
he was familiar   Once these possessors of recently acquired wealth
departed from the accepted rules of the game and began to drive
toward the accomplishment of their own ends, be the cost what it
might, the old order was doomed.   Some other form of representation would soon become imperative.

  This interpretation has the merit of relieving Robinson of the
opprobrium of hypocrisy, a fault of which there is no other reason
to accuse him.   It explains, too, the insistence with which historians
have stipulated that this election had a different character from
those in the generations preceding it.   It was different ; a new
force appeared in 1784 definitely organized for the purpose of taking
a part it had not played in like manner before   This force was not
an aroused populace, indignant at a corrupt bargain between Fox
and North, but a group of commercial magnates in desperate terror
of the coalition because they felt that its policies endangered their
property and their privileges.   Once this force realized that it was
able to become a potent factor in politics, the *dénouement* of 1832
was in prospect.   The terror incidental to the Revolutionary and
Napoleonic wars delayed the change, but it was unreasonable to
expect either these magnates or the industrial capitalists who were
following in their wake to be satisfied with the complicated processes
of election so familiar to Robinson.

  That Robinson was little inclined to see the defects in the existing
order is evident from the genuine pleasure he seems to have found
in establishing a family interest in Monmouthshire for his son-in-law
as illustrated in the Appendix to this volume by letters selected
from those that he wrote to Henry Nevill. Unfortunately the
limits of this volume would not permit the printing of the entire
collection of letters.   They afford an insight into the character
of Robinson not perceptible in the parliamentary papers, and they
are, besides, illuminating relics of the social history of his time.

  Of the papers in the fourth section of the volume, little needs to
be added here to the notes in which they are severally described

and introduced. The correspondence at the time of the payment of North's debts by the king merely fills in details of a curious story. Neither the " little red book of accounts " nor the list of receipts for secret service funds add much except confirmatory details to the knowledge, now common, concerning the political methods prevalent in Robinson's time. These items, therefore, lose much of the importance that Mr. Stevens attached to them when he found them. The moderateness of the sums involved rather than the amount impresses us most. These papers by no means give evidence that George III and his ministers indulged in the practice of bribery and corruption in the degree that has sometimes been alleged. Probably few members of parliament would have tolerated anything as crude as open bribery even in that time. In any case, bribery would have been a much more costly method of obtaining a majority than that actually used, namely the much surer process of procuring the choice of members of the House of Commons on whom the government of the day could depend and of binding them to give support by the hundreds of favours it was in the power of the king and his ministers to grant. Money was essential for election purposes, and that in sums of considerable size, but the purposes for which it was used were, for the most part, conventional at the time and were not regarded by the members of the ruling class as corrupt practices.[1]

We have ample evidence that George III was zealous in his efforts to procure the return of parliaments friendly to his theories of the royal prerogative and disposed to support him in his struggle with the Whigs. For that purpose he stinted himself in his personal expenditure in order that the funds available from the secret service might be increased by his personal contributions. But the funds so provided were used for purposes differing little from those regularly practised by all parties. The theory of kingship upheld by George III is radically different from that now accepted for a British monarch, but there is not much to show that he supported that theory by more corrupt practices than were used by the Whig magnates in opposing it. If he was able to spend money somewhat more freely than they, it was because, having access to the public purse for a greater proportion of the period of the struggle, he had larger sums to spend, not because he had fewer scruples about spending it. Finally, the forces that began to be potent in the general election of 1784 were destined ultimately to make the sums used

[1] W.H. 1774.

by both George III and the Whigs seem paltry and almost insigni-
ficant in comparison with their lavish expenditure.[1]

The task of preparing these papers for publication has been the
more difficult in that the editor has never seen the originals. He
has had to depend entirely on copies made by or under the supervision of the late Mr. B. F. Stevens. He ought to say, in gratitude
to Mr. Stevens, that the task, difficult as it has been in places, was
much facilitated by the care with which the copying seems to have
been done. There may be, of course, faults in the finished work
chargeable to the copyist ; there may be others for which the editor
is to blame His aim, however, has been to reproduce the copy as
made by Mr. Stevens except as regards abbreviation, capitalization,
and punctuation. In these matters he has taken the liberty of
using his discretion, never of course making a change that would,
make a material difference in the sense of the text.

It has not seemed wise to reproduce any portion of the paper read
by Mr. Stevens at the Royal Historical Society in 1891 when he first
exploited these documents. Portions of the letter of Mr. Stevens to
the Marquess of Abergavenny, in which he describes these and other
papers found during his search at Eridge Castle, are printed as an
Appendix Mr. Stevens apparently contemplated the publication
of the materials printed in this volume in the form of a sort
of digest of political methods, arranged according to the parliamentary constituencies. This method of arrangement did not
seem wise to the present editor, who has thought it best to print
the papers as Robinson left them, arranging them for the most
part in chronological order, leaving them to tell their own story.

There is due to Mr. Stevens, however, a debt of gratitude from all
students of British political history in the eighteenth century for
his labour in making these papers available for public use, and to the
Marquess of Abergavenny a similar debt for giving him access to
them and permission to publish them.

The editor acknowledges his own indebtedness to Dr. Hubert
Hall, Director of the Royal Historical Society, for helpful suggestions at every stage of his work and for reading the proofs.

WILLIAM THOMAS LAPRADE. ·

---

[1] The Editor is indebted to the Rev. W. Hunt's edition of the electoral
propaganda relating to "The Irish Parliament of 1775" (1907) for an in-
structive analogy.

THE PARLIAMENTARY ELECTION
OF 1774

SECTION I

THE PARLIAMENTARY ELECTION OF 1774

THE following statements appear on an elaborately tabulated diagram which it does not seem worth while to reproduce since this could not be done easily on pages the size of the volume. The paper is endorsed in Robinson's hand : " Abstract of State and supposed cases as first drawn out on the Royal Marriage Bill " The division on the final vote on this bill, the last of a number of divisions in the debate, which took place in March, 1772, is given in the Parliamentary History, (XVII, 424), as 168 to 115 in its favour. Other divisions were better attended than this; the figures on one question were 268 to 140.

Pro present 249; pro sent for 19; pro sick, present 6; pro sick, absent 2; pro absent 15; from which it appears : pro supposed may attend 268, total pro sick 8; making a total of 276 pro, suppose all to be got that possibly can, which, together with 15 absentees that can't be got, make 291 total friends.

Con present 162; con may attend 8; con sick, present 3, con sick, absent 2; con absent 8; from which it appears : con supposed may attend 170; total con sick 5; making a total of 175 con, suppose all to be got that is possible, which, taken with 8 absentees that cannot be got, make 183 total opponents

Doubtful present 71; doubtful sick, present 1; doubtful sick, absent 1; doubtful absent 8; making a total of 71 doubtful that may attend; 2 doubtful sick; which, taken together, make 73 doubtful, suppose all the doubtful to attend that can be got, which, with the 8 doubtful absent, make a total doubtful of 81.

The totals in these three classes with 2 vacant seats and the Speaker make the 558 members of the house

Suppose all our friends attend that can be got, there would be 276 ; suppose all their friends whatever attend, there would be 183 ; suppose all the doubtful attend against, there would be 81 ; a total against of 264 ; majority in that case would be 12

Suppose all our friends attend that can be got, there would be 276 ; suppose we have out of the doubtful only 21 ; we would have 297 ; suppose all their friends whatever attend, there would be 183 ; allow them of the doubtful 60 ; they would have in all 243 ; majority in this case 54.

Suppose all our friends attend that can be got, there would be 276 ; suppose we have of the doubtful 40 ; we would have 316 ; suppose all their friends whatsoever attend, there would be 183 ; allow them of the doubtful 41 ; they would have 224 ; majority in this case 92

Suppose friends which it's thought may be got, there would be 268 ; allow all their friends whatsoever to attend, there would be 183 ; allow all the doubtful whatever to attend for them, there would be 81 ; they would have 264 ; majority in this case 4

Suppose friends attend which it's thought may be got, there would be 268 ; opponents that may attend, there would be 175 ; allow them all the doubtful to attend that it is thought can, there would be 73 ; they would have 248 ; majority in this case 20

Suppose only our friends attend which it's imagined will be got, there would be 268 ; suppose we have only out of the doubtful 21 ; we would have 289 ; allow all their friends whatsoever to attend, there would be 183 ; allow them out of the doubtful 60 , they would have 243 ; majority in this case 46.

Suppose friends attend which it's thought may be got, there would be 268 ; suppose we have of the doubtful that may attend 36 ; we would have 304 ; allow all their friends whatsoever to attend, there would be 183 ; allow them out of the doubtful 37 ; they would have 220 ; majority in this case 84

Suppose friends attend which it's thought may be got, there would be 268 ; suppose we have half the doubtful that can attend, there would be 36 ; we would have in all 304 ; suppose opponents to attend which it's thought may be got, there would be 175 ; allow them of the doubtful that it's thought can attend 37 ; they would have in all 212 ; majority in this case 92.

The following memoranda are dated December 13, 1773, and were obviously made in anticipation of a general parliamentary election. Whether an earlier dissolution than took place was under consideration or Robinson was merely making ready in advance for an undertaking that could not be postponed much longer is not known. Nor is there evidence in the transcript to indicate whether these minutes were prepared by Robinson himself or were prepared for him by some other person. The election of 1774 was the first general election in the administrations of both Robinson and North, and Scotland was not yet as well organized as it later became under the management of Henry Dundas.

MINUTES AS TO SCOTLAND.

[Seat]	[Member, 1768–74]	[New Parliament]
Orkney's	Thomas Dundas, Jr., Esq.	Most likely the same.
Caithness .	. . . .	Not send this time, but *Bute*.[1]
Sutherland	Hon. James Weemyss	Same. If like to quit, to either Grant for Sutherland or Lord Seaforth for the borough.
Kirkwall	⎫	Is Sir L[awrence] Dundas's, who has given it to General Scot for some time, who is connected with Governor Grant and joins with Weemyss in bringing Grant in.
Wick . .	⎪ Governor Grant . .	Is in private hands, but would go with Mr. Mackenzie for Lord Seaforth.
Dornock .	⎪	Is Mr. Weemyss', who joins General Scot for Grant.
Tain . .	⎪	Is Mr. David Ross's, and would go with Mr. Mackenzie.
Dingwall .	⎭	Is a Mr. Mackenzie's of Delvie's, a friend of Governor Grant's.
Ross . .	Mr. Mackenzie . .	Same, or Lord Seaforth.
Cromartie	William Pulteney .	Not send this time, but Nairn does.
Nairn . .	. . . .	Cosmo Gordon, an Advocate at Edinburgh
Inverness County	General Fraser . .	Query, Promise last time to the Duke of Gordon. If exacted, can't well stand

---

[1] Bute and Caithness, like several other groups of Scotch constituencies sent members to parliament alternately. Caithness had elected the member in 1768, so it would be Bute's turn at the next election.

		again, and if not one of the Gordon family will come in, or perhaps *Lord Seaforth* ; the independant gentlemen for him and for Fraser and against the Duke of Gordon.
Fortrose, Inverness, Nairn, and Forres }	Colonel Monro . .	Same again.
Elgin County	General Grant	A contest by Mr Duff against *General Grant* doubtful ; Monro, it is said, can cast the scale.
Banff County	Lord Fife . . .	Same again, but as he contests Elgin he may have trouble here by the Grants, and it is said he is not certain. Lord Pitfour. Mr Ferguson can cast the scale Lord Gordon now opposes Lord Fife violently.
Aberdeen- shire .	Mr Garden . .	Same again
Elgin . . }		Is between Lord Finlater and Sir James Grant and the Duke of Gordon.
Cullin . .		Is Lord Finlater.
Banf . .	Thomas Lockhart	Is part Lord Findlatter's and Mr. Garden's and some other private persons.
Inverury and		Is principally Mr. Burnets.
Kintore . }		Is chiefly Lord Marshall's and managed by Mr Burnet. It is uncertain who will come in next time. Some say young Burnet will stand, others that Mr. Lockhart is to come in again.
Kincardin County	Mr Hepburn .	New one. Lord Adam Gordon, to whom this county hath been offered by the gentlemen
Angus County .	Lord Panmure . .	Same again.
Aberdeen }		Is independent among several gentlemen, but chiefly government.
Inverbervy		Lord Arbuthnot's ; said now to be secured by Lord Strathmore.
Brechin . }	Mr. Lyon .	Lord Panmure's.
Montrose and Aberbro- thock . }		James Aberdeen.
		Lord Panmure's.
Perth County	Colonel Murray . .	Same again supposed, but there will be strong opposition by Mr. Graham, who is supported by Mr. Douglas who has split his estate and made many votes.

Fortar Dundee Perth Coupar St Andrews }	} Mr. Dempster .	These boroughs are very open, venal, and expensive, and few chuse to engage with them. Government has a good interest among them, many places to be given, being ports, and many placemen, but no one has yet started.
Fife County	General Scott .	Same again.
Crail, Kilrenny, Anstruther, East and West, Pittenween }	} Sir John Anstruther M[one]y . . .	S[ir] J[ohn] is abroad, and Query, yet whether he will come in again.
Dysart, Kircaldy, Kinghorn, and Burnt Island }	} Mr. Oswald .	Same again. The boroughs mostly his by management and places.
Kinross	Mr. Adam . .	Kinross does not send this next time, but——
County Clackmannan.	. . . .	A contest. Lieutenant Colonel Abercombie is one of the candidates and has Sir L[awrence] Dundas's support Captain Erskine, an officer in the Guards of the Mar family, is another candidate and has considerable interest of his own, and, it is said, will carry it.
Stirlingshire	Mr. Thomas Dundas	A contest. Sir James Campbell opposes Mr. Dundas an old family interest, Sir James having represented the county before, and warmly supported
Stirling, Culross, Dumferling, Inverkeithing, and Queensferry }	} Mr. Masterton . .	A contest. Colonel A[rchibald] Campbell. M[one]y. Government.
Dumbarton County .	Sir Archibald Edmonstone . .	Same again.
Dumbarton, Glasgow, Renfrew, Rutheglen }	} Lord F[rederick] Campbell .	Same again. Government.
Renfrew County .	Mr. Macdowal . .	New. Mr. John Crawford.
Bute County	None now . . .	Lord Bute. One of his sons, it is said, is to come in. Mr. James Stuart.

Iverary,
Campbel- } . . . . . . These are the Duke of Argyles.
town, }
         Mr. James Stuart[1]
Rothsay, } . . . . Lord Bute's
Irwin, and } . Lord Eglintoun's if any persons.
Air . } . . Lord Loudoun chiefly, if any one is.
Air County   Mr. Kennedy . Supposed same again, though said to be opposed by Sir Adam Ferguson who stands against the peers : Cassils, Loudon, and Eglington.

Lanerk   Captain   L[ockhar]t Supposed will stand again. Hamilton
County   Ross   and Douglas families have great interest in this county and will probably be opposite to each other. Mr Campbell of Shawfield will perhaps be a candidate. Mr. Andrew Stuart has also been talked of.

Lanerk } . . . . . Mr. Douglas and Mr Murray of Cringelty.
Linlithgow } . The Hamiltons, but m[one]y
      } Sir James Cockburn And supposed he may come in again.
Peebles } . . . Lord March, but m[one]y.
Selkirk } . . . M[one]y. Duke of Buccleugh. Captain Lockhart Ross talked of to stand.

Linlithgow   Mr. James Dundas . Will not come in again. Lord Hopeton
County   the principal interest, and therefore who he pleases ; perhaps Sir William Cunningham.

Midlothian   Sir A[lexander] Gil- Thought will not come in again, being
County   mour   opposed by Mr. Solicitor Dundas who, it is apprehended, will carry it.

Edinburgh   Sir L[awrence] Dundas Who government pleases Query, State of the magistracy.

Hadding-   Sir George Suttie It is said that there will be a contest.
toun   Sir George Suttie says he is secure.
County   Mr. Stuart, Officer of the Guards, Lord Blantyre's brother.

North }
  Berwick, }
Dunbar, }
Hadding- } Sir Patrick Warrender Who, it is supposed, will come in again.
toun, }   But it is said he will be opposed
Lander, }
Jedburgh . } . . . . N.B. This borough is at present disqualified

---

[1] In the transcript before the "Lord Bute's," which clearly refers to Rothsay, appears on the same line with "Mr. James Stuart," "Same again or Sir George Macartney" with the "Same again or" drawn through

Peebles County	Lord Advocate . .	Same again.
Selkirk County	John Pringle . .	Same again.
Roxburgh County	Sir Gilbert Elliot .	Same again.
Dumfries County	General Douglas .	Will go out. Probably Major Laurie. Sir James Johnstone has declared, that he will stand.
Sanquhar, Lochmaben, Dumfries, Annan, Kircud-bright	Mr. William Douglas.	Probably same again. Duke of Queens-bury.
Kircudbright County	Mr. Murray . . .	Will not come in again ; said Mr. Heron will stand.
Galloway County	Captain Keith Stewart.	Supposed same again.
Wigtoun, Whitehorn, New Gallo-way, Stranwaer	William Stewart. .	Said that Lord Stairs will oppose.

The following papers are classified with others relating to the parliamentary election of 1774, the first general election after Robinson became Secretary to the Treasury, because from their date and character they were apparently prepared by or for Robinson for use in that canvass. The papers are undated, but internal evidence fixes their date between March 12, 1774, and the dissolution of parliament in that year.

LIST OF OFFICES TENABLE WITH SEATS IN LORDS AND COMMONS.

Groom of the Stole ; 13 Lords of the Bedchamber ; 11 Grooms. of the Bedchamber ; Privy Purse ; 4 Gentlemen Ushers Privy Chamber ; 4 Gentlemen Ushers, Daily Waiters ; Master of the Ceremonies ; Master of the Robes ; Master of the Jewel Office ; Yeoman and Clerk of the Jewel Office ; Groom Porter ; Housekeeper at Whitehall ; 24 Rangers, Keepers, Out Rangers, and Deputy

Rangers of Parks and Forests ; Surveyor General of Woods and Parks ; Surveyor General of Crown Lands ; Master of the Harriers ; Master of the Buckhounds ; Master of the Staghounds ; Master Falconer ; Keeper of the Great Wardrobe ; Deputy to the Keeper of the Great Wardrobe ; Comptroller of the Great Wardrobe ; Patent Clerk ; Lord Steward, Household ; Treasurer ; Comptroller ; Cofferer , Deputy Cofferer ; Clerk Venison Warrants ; Master of Household ; 3 Clerks Comptrollers Green Cloth ; Letter Carrier to the King ; *Query*, Clerk Comptroller Kitchen ; Captain of the Band of Pensioners ; *Query*, Lieutenant of the Band of Pensioners ; Captain of the Yeomen of the Guard ; *Query*, Lieutenant of the Yeomen of the Guard ; Master of the Horse Avenor and Clerk Marshall ; 7 Equerries ; Surveyor General of the Board of Works ; Comptroller of the Board of Works ; Surveyor of Private Roads ; Paymaster of the Works ; Surveyor of Gardens and Waters ; Lord Warden of the Stannaries ; Surveyor-General of Cornwall ; Auditor of the Dutchy of Cornwall ; Receiver General of the Dutchy of Cornwall ; Treasurer of the Chamber ; Lord Chamberlain to the Queen ; Vice Chamberlain to the Queen ; 3 Gentlemen Ushers of Private Chambers ; 3 Gentlemen Ushers, Daily Waiters ; Treasurer to the Queen ; Secretary to the Queen ; Comptroller to the Queen ; Attorney General to the Queen ; Sollicitor General ; Master of the Horse ; 3 Equerries ; 23 Ambassadors and Ministers and their Secretaries abroad ; 5 Lords of the Treasury ; 2 Secretaries ; Auditor of the Exchequer ; Clerk of the Pells ; 4 Tellers ; 2 Chamberlains of the Stally Court ; Usher of the Exchequer ; 2 Auditors of the Imprest ; Auditor for several Counties in England for Life ; Auditor for the Principality of Wales ; Paymaster of Pensions , Lord Chancellor ; Master of Rolls ; 12 Masters in Chancery ; Clerk of the Crown ; Master of the Hanaper , Keeper of Records in the Tower ; Curtos Brevium, Common Pleas ; Chirographer ; Secretary to the Chancellor of the Exchequer , Remembrancer ; Clerk of the Pipe ; Remembrancer of First Fruits Office ; Comptroller of First Fruits and Tenths ; Chief Justice of Chester ; 7 Welch (*sic*) Judges ; Attorney General ; Sollicitor General ; 5 King's Serjeants ; 21 King's Council and Serjeants ; Chancellor of the Dutchy of Lancaster ; Attorney General to the Dutchy of Lancaster ; King's Serjeant in the Dutchy of Lancaster ; 2 King's Council in the Dutchy of Lancaster ; Attorney General and Serjeant of the County Palatine of Lancaster ;

Clerk of the Crown to the County Palatine of Lancaster ; Principal of the Arches Court of Canterbury ; Advocate General ; Lord Privy Seal ; *Query*, Decypherer ; 3 Secretaries of State , 6 Under Secretaries , *Query*, Law Clerk to Ditto ; 6 Lords of Trade ; Secretary to the Lords of Trade , Council to the Lords of Trade ; Postmaster General of Peers ; 7 Lords of the Admiralty ; 2 Secretaries to Ditto ; Judge of the Admiralty Court ; Council to Ditto and Navy ; Treasurer of the Navy ; Comptroller of the Navy ; Master of Greenwich Hospital ; *Query*, Lieutenant Governor of Greenwich Hospital , Admirals of the Navy ; Captains of the Navy ; Secretary at War ; *Query*, Deputy to Secretary at War , Paymaster General ; Deputy Paymaster General ; Master of the Ordnance ; Lieutenant General of the Ordnance ; Surveyor General of the Ordnance , Clerk of the Ordnance ; Storekeeper of the Ordnance ; Clerk of the Deliveries ; Treasurer and Paymaster ; Comptroller of the Laboratory at Woolwich ; Chief Engineer and Colonel of the Military Branch ; Governor of Chelsea Hospital ; Lieutenant Governor of Chelsea Hospital ; Clerk of the Works ; Constable of the Tower ; Lieutenant Governor of the Tower ; 33 Governments of Garrisons ; 28 Lieutenant Governors of Garrisons ; Adjutant General , Deputy Adjutant General ; Quartermaster General , Deputy to the Quartermaster General ; 2 Comptrollers of Army Accounts ; Commander in Chief in Great Britain , Adjutant General to Great Britain , Commissary of Musters ; Barrack Master ; 60 Lieutenancys of Counties

Scotland : Keeper of the Great Seal , Lord Privy Seal , Lord Register ; Vice Admiral ; Lord Justice General , Lord President , Lord Advocate ; Lord Justice Clerk , Keeper of the Signet , Lord High Constable , Heritable Keeper of the King's Household , Heritable Usher of Parliament ; Keeper of Holyrood House ; Keeper of Falkland , Keeper of Scoon ; Keeper of Lockmaben , Keeper of Dunstafnage and Carrick ; Keeper of Linlithgow , Master of the Works , President of Police ; 4 Lords of Police.

Ireland : Lord Lieutenant ; Secretary to the Lord Lieutenant ; Lord High Treasurer ; 3 Vice Treasurers ; Chancellor of the Exchequer ; Chief Remembrancer , Clerk of Pells ; Clerk of the Council ; Constable of Dublin Castle ; Keepers of the Phenix Park ; Master General of Ordnance, Civil Branch ; Lieutenant General of Ordnance ; *Query*, Several other employments in Ireland.

LIST OF PEERS WHO HOLD OFFICES.

Duke of Grafton : Lord Privy Seal ; Duke of Beaufort : Lieutenancy ; Duke of St. Albans : Grand Falconer and Lieutenancy ; Duke of Bolton : Vice Admiral of Southampton and Dorset and Admiral ; Duke of Devonshire : Lord High Treasurer of Ireland and Governor of Corke ; Duke of Marlborough : Lieutenancy ; Duke of Queensbury : Lord Justice General in Scotland ; Duke of Ancaster : Master of the Horse and a Lieutenancy ; Duke of Manchester Collector of Customs, Outwards, and Lieutenancy ; Duke of Chandos : Lieutenancy and Ranger of Endfield ; Duke of Dorset : Vice Admiral of the Coasts and Lieutenancy ; Duke of Newcastle : Auditor of the Exchequer, Comptroller of Customs, Lieutenancy ; Duke of Northumberland : Lieutenancy ; Duke of Montague : Governor of Windsor Castle ; Marquis of Rockingham : Lieutenancy ; Earl of Derby : Lieutenancy ; Earl Pembroke : Lord of the Bedchamber, Colonel of the First Regiment Dragoons, a Lieutenancy ; Earl of Suffolk : Secretary of State ; Earl of Exeter · Lieutenancy , Earl of Northampton Lieutenancy ; Earl of Denbigh : Lord of the Bedchamber, Master of the Harriers and Fox Hounds , Earl of Sandwich : First Lord of the Admiralty , Earl of Litchfield : Curtos Brevium of Common Pleas ; Earl of Berkley : Constable of St. Bruvel's Castle in the Forest of Dean, Lieutenancy ; Earl of Holderness : Governor of Prince of Wales, Etc., Lord Warden of the Cinque Ports, Governor of Dover Castle for Life, Lieutenancy ; Earl of Scarborough : Deputy Earl Marshal of England ; Earl of Rochford : Secretary of State, Vice Admiral of the Coast, and a Lieutenancy ; Earl of Coventry : Lieutenancy ; Earl of Jersey : Lord of Bedchamber ; Earl Powlett : Lieutenancy , Earl of Cholmondeley : Lieutenancy ; Earl of Oxford Lord of Bedchamber ; Earl of Ferrers · Captain in the Navy , Earl of Dartmouth Secretary of State, First Lord of Trade ; Earl of Bristol · Groom of the Stole ; Earl of Pomfret : Lord of the Bedchamber and Keeper of the Tower Parks at Windsor ; Duke of Roxburgh : Lord of the Bedchamber ; Earl of Waldegrave : Master of the Horse to the Queen and Colonel of the Coldstream Regiment ; Earl of Ashburnham : Keeper of the Great Wardrobe ; Earl of Effingham : Captain in the Army ; Earl of Oxford : Ranger of St. James and Hyde Parks, Lord of Bedchamber, Curtos Rotulorum ; Earl of Harrington : Colonel of the Second Troop of Horse Grenadier

Guards, Comptroller of Customs—Dublin ; Earl Gower : Lord President and Curtos Rotulorum ; Earl of Buckinghamshire · Lord of Bedchamber ; Earl Harcourt : Lord Lieutenant of Ireland ; Earl of Hertford : Lord Chamberlain, Curtos Rotulorum ; Earl of Guilford : Treasurer to the Queen ; Earl Cornwallis : Constable of the Tower, Colonel of the 33 Regiment ; Earl of Hardwicke : Teller of the Exchequer, Lieutenancy ; Earl of Darlington : Master of the Jewel Office, Governor of Carlisle, Lord Lieutenant and Vice Admiral of the County of Durham ; Earl of Ilchester : Joint Comptroller of Army Accounts ; Earl Delaware : Colonel of the First Troop of Horse Guards and Lord Chamberlain to the Queen , Earl Talbot : Lord Steward ; Earl of Northington . Master of the Hanaper and Teller of the Exchequer , Earl of Hillsborough : Register (?) Court Chancery in Ireland ; Lord Viscount Townshend Master General of the Ordnance, Colonel the Queen's Regiment of Dragoons , Lord Viscount Bolingbroke : Lord Bedchamber ; Lord Viscount Falmouth : Captain of the Yeomen of the Guard , Lord Le Despencer : Joint Postmaster General, Lieutenancy ; Lord Ferrers : Lieutenant Dragoons in Ireland ; Lord Willoughby : Lord Bedchamber ; Lord Masham : Lord Bedchamber and Remembrancer Exchequer ; Lord Cadogan : Colonel Second Troop Horse Guards, Governor of Gravesend and Tilbury Fort ; Lord Godolphin : Governor of Scilly Islands ; Lord Edgecumbe : Captain of the Band of Gentlemen Pensioners ; Lord Bruce : Lord Bedchamber , Lord Ponsonby : Vice Admiral of Munster in Ireland , Lord Hyde : Chancellor of the Duchy of Lancaster , Lord Mansfield : Chief Justice of King's Bench ; Lord Sondes : Auditor of the Imprest—Life ; Lord Grantham : Ambassador to Spain ; Lord Pelham : Chief Justice in Eyre and Surveyor General of the Customs , Lord Holland : Clerk of the Pells in Ireland for Life , Lord Ducie : Clerk Crown Court Palatine of Lancaster ; Lord Digby : Lieutenancy ; Duke of Argyle : Commander in Chief in Scotland , Lord Apsley : Lord Chancellor.

Scots Peers.

Duke of Gordon : Captain in Army ; Marquis of Lothian · Colonel of Dragoons ; Earl of Errol : Lord High Constable of Scotland , Earl of Loudoun : Governor of Edinburgh Castle and Colonel of Third Regiment of Foot Guards ; Earl of Dunmore :

Governor of Virginia ; Earl of March Vice Admiral of Scotland and Lord of the Bedchamber ; Earl of Marchmont : Keeper of the Great Seal in Scotland ; Earl of Bute : Ranger of Richmond Park ; Lord Stormount : Ambassador to France ; Lord Cathcart : Lord High Commissioner of the General Assembly of the Church of Scotland, First Lord Commissioner of Police.

LIST OF MEMBERS OF THE HOUSE OF COMMONS WHO HOLD OFFICES, COMMANDS, CONTRACTS, LIEUTENANCIES, OR GOVERNMENTS.

Sir Richard Sutton : Council to the Board of Ordnance ; Sir J[ohn] Griffin : A Troop of Horse Grenadier Guards ; General Honeywood : A Regiment ; Sir George Colebroke : Remembrancer of the First Fruits ; Anthony Bacon : Contract ; John Durand : Contract ; Lord North : Treasury ; J[ohn] Clevland : Accomptant of Sixpenny Office ; Sir J[ohn] Selbright A Regiment ; Richard Vernon : Clerk of the Green Cloth ; Alexander Wedderburn : Sollicitor General ; General [Henry] Clinton : A Regiment ; Lord Mounstuart Lieutanancy , Sir G[eorge] Osborn : Groom of the Bedchamber ; Lord Robert Bertie Lord of the Bedchamber and a Regiment ; William Egerton : Clerk of the Jewel Office and Major in the Horse Guards ; T[imothy] Caswell : Deputy Paymaster of the Forces ; Charles Ambler : Sollicitor General to the Queen ; Lord Clare : Vice Treasurer , T[homas] Whitmore : Major in the Ninth Regiment of Foot ; T[homas] Worsley : Surveyor General of the Works ; T[homas] Townshend : Teller of the Exchequer ; C[harles] S[loane] Cadogan : Master of the Mint ; S[oame] Jenyns : Lord of Trade ; Sir W[illiam] Lynch : Foreign Minister ; Lord Lisburne : Lord of the Admiralty ; George Rice . Treasurer of the Chamber ; Sir S[?] Wynn : Auditor of Wales ; Glyn Wynn · A Company in the Guards , W[illiam] Keppel : A Regiment ; Sir E[dward] Baynton : Surveyor General of Cornwall , J[ames] Harris : Secretary to the Queen ; J[ames] Harris, junior : Foreign Minister ; Sir J[ames] Lowther Lieutenancy , J[ohn] Jenkinson · Gentleman Usher to the Queen and a Captain in the Army ; H[enry] S[eymour] Conway, junior : Constable of Dublin Castle and Clerk of the Crown in Ireland ; R[ichard] Hopkins : Clerk of the Green · Cloth ; Sir L[ynch] [Salusbury] Cotton : Receiver General of the Rents in N[orth] Wales ; R[ichard] Myddleton : Lieutenancy ; Lord George Cavendish : Lieutenancy ; Lord F[rederick] Cavendish :

A Regiment ; Sir J[oseph] Yorke : Foreign Minister ; J[ames] Hayes : Welch Judge ; J[ohn] Lambton : A Regiment ; J[ames] Buller : Lord of the Admiralty ; General [Charles] Fitzroy : Vice Chancellor to the Queen and a Regiment ; R[ichard] B[urton] Phillipson . Lieutenant Colonel of a Regiment of Dragoons ; Sir R[oger] Mostyn : Lieutenancy ; Benjamin Langton : Colonel of Ordnance ; G[eorge] Selwyn · Paymaster of the Works, Surveyor of the Mint, Etc ; G[rey] Cooper : Secretary to the Treasury ; C[harles] W[olfran] Cornwall : Lord of the Treasury ; F[raser] C[ottayne] Cust : Council to Admiralty ; A[nthony] St. Leger : Colonel in the Army , J[ohn] Irwin : A Regiment ; Sir F[letcher] Norton : Speaker, Chief Justice of Eyre ; G[eorge] Onslow : Out Ranger of Windsor Forest ; Sir S[imeon] Stuart · Chamberlain of Talley Court ; E[dward] Harvey : Adjutant General and a Regiment , C[harles] Jenkinson : Vice Treasurer ; T[homas] M[ore] Molyneux : Company of Guards , W[illiam] Ashburnham : Deputy Keeper of the Wardrobe ; W[illiam] Evelyn : A Regiment ; [James Hamilton], Earl of Clanbrassil : Remembrancer in Ireland ; Charles F[itzroy] Scudamore : Deputy Ranger of Whittlebury ; W[illiam] A'Court : A Regiment ; J[ames] Wallace : King's Council and Attorney General of Durham and Lancaster ; [John], Viscount Hinchinbroke : Vice Chamberlain to the Queen ; Peter Legh : An Office held, part of which for him ; Lord R[obert] Manners : A Regiment and a Lieutenant Government ; H[umphry] Morrice : Lord Warden ; W[illiam] Amherst : A Company in the Guards ; Sir E[yre] Coote : A Regiment ; [John Bateman], Lord Bateman : Master of the Buck Hounds ; E[dward] Elliot : Lord of Trade ; H[enry] Fane : Surveyor of Roads ; T[homas] Gilbert . Comptroller of the Wardrobe and Paymaster of Pensions to Widows of Sea Officers ; Sir W[illiam] Meredith : Comptroller of the Household ; T[homas] Harley : A Contract ; Sir H[enry] Burrard · A Government , H[enry] Meynell : Master of the Stag Hounds ; C[harles] Rainsford : Deputy Lieutenant of the Tower and in the Army and Aid du Camp ; J[ames] Brudenell . Master of the Robes ; G[eorge] Boscawen : Lieutenant in the Horse Guards ; J[ohn] Stephenson : A Contract ; Colonel [Henry Lawes] Luttrell . Lieutenant Colonel of Horse and Adjutant General for Ireland ; Sir C[harles] Whitworth : A Lieutenant Government ; J[ohn] Manners : Housekeeper at Whitehall ; Sir J[ohn] Shelley : Treasurer of the Household ; G[eorge] Hay : Dean of the Arches ; H[ans]

Sloane : Deputy Cofferer ; Sir G[eorge Bridges] Rodney : Rear Admiral of Great Britain ; W[illiam] Howe : A Regiment ; R[ichard] Fitzpatrick : A Lieutenant in the Guards ; [Francis Seymour Conway], Viscount Beauchamp : Lord of the Treasury ; R[obert Seymour] Conway : Captain of Dragoons ; Lord C[harles] Spencer : Lord of the Admiralty ; Colonel [William] Harcourt : Groom of the Bedchamber and Lieutenant Colonel in the Army ; Lord R[obert] Spencer : Lord of Trade ; Captain [Hugh ?] Pigot : Company of Marines ; W[illiam] Jollyffe : Lord of Trade ; W[elbore] Ellis : Vice Treasurer ; [William Wildman], Viscount Barrington : Secretary at War ; Sir C[harles] Hardy : Master of Greenwich Hospital ; T[homas] Calcraft : Lieutenant-Colonel in the Army ; J[ohn] Burgoyne : A Regiment and a Governor ; Sir C[harles] Frederick : Colonel in the Army, Surveyor General of Ordnance ; Chase Price : An Office held for him ; E[dward] Lewis : A Contract ; W[illiam] Norton : Minister to the Swiss Cantons ; W[illiam] [Aislabie ?] : Auditor of Imprests ; R[ichard] Jackson : Council to the Board of Trade ; J[ohn] Morton : Chief Justice of Chester ; G[eorge] B[ridges] Brudenell : Clerk Comptroller of the Green Cloth ; John Norris : Governor of Deal Castle ; John Yorke : Clerk of the Crown, Etc. ; Sir C[harles] Cocks : Clerk of the Deliveries in Ordnance ; T[homas] Bradshaw : Lord of the Admiralty ; P[hilip] Stephens : Secretary to the Admiralty ; W[illiam] G[erard] Hamilton : Chancellor of the Exchequer in Ireland ; Lord Gage : Paymaster of Pensions ; Peregrine Cust : A Contract ; Robert, Lord Clive : A Lieutenancy ; [Henry], Lord Palmerston : Lord of the Admiralty ; H[enry] Stanley : Governor of the Isle of Wight ; Sir J[ohn] Wrottesley : A Company in the Guards ; G[eorge] Howard : A Regiment and a Government ; G[eorge] Onslow : Lord of the Treasury ; Lord G[eorge] Lennox : A Regiment ; E[dward] Thurlow : Attorney General ; General [Charles] Vernon : Deputy Lieutenant of the Tower ; R[ichard] Rigby : Paymaster of the Forces ; General [Henry Seymour] Conway : A Regiment and a Government ; [Charles Stanhope], Lord Petersham : In the Guards ; P[eter] Burrell : Surveyor General of Lands ; J[ohn] Grey : Clerk of the Green Cloth ; General [George] Boscawen : A Regiment and a Lieutenant Government ; W[hitshed] Keene : Lord of Trade ; C[harles] Greville : Lord of Trade ; B[amber] Gascoyne : Lord of Trade ; C[harles] Dillon : Deputy Ranger of Hampton Court Park ; Earl Percy : A Regiment ; J[ohn] Robinson : Secretary to the Admiralty [Treasury ?][1] ; J[eremiah] Dyson : Cofferer ; J[ohn] Tucker : Paymaster of the Marines ; N[icholas] Herbert : Secretary of Jamaica ; A[rnold] Nisbett : A Contract ; H[enry] Penton : Letter Carrier ; [George] Powlett : Groom Porter ; W[illiam] Gordon : Lieutenant Colonel in the Army ; J[ohn] Skynner : Welch Judge ; H[enry] St. John : Groom of the Bedchamber and in the Army ; C[harles] Townshend : Lord of the Treasury ; General [John] Parker : A Regiment , J[ohn] Pringle : Master of the Works in Scotland ; R[obert] Adam · Clerk of the Works to Chelsea Hospital ; Sir A[rchibald] Edmondstone : An Office held in part for him ; General [Archibald] Douglas : A Regiment ; J[ames] Masterton : Barrack Master in Scotland ; Sir P[atrick] Warrender : Remembrancer in Scotland and Lieutenant Colonel in the Army ; Sir A[lexander] Gilmour : Clerk of Green Cloth ; General [Francis] Grant · A Regiment ; J[ohn] Scott : A Regiment ; [William Maule], Earl Panmure . A Regiment ; J[ames] Townshend Oswald : Secretary and Clerk to Leeward Islands ; J[ames] Montgomery · Lord Advocate ; D[avid] Graeme : A Regiment ; J[ames] S[tuart] Mackenzie : Lord Privy Seal ; Sir G[ilbert] Elliot . Treasurer of the Navy ; Lord F[rederick] Campbell : Lord Register.

The following minutes, dated June 30, 1774, concern only those constituencies in Scotland where contests were likely in the prospective general election Six months of gathering information enabled Robinson, or whoever prepared the minutes, to be more definite in statement than was the case in the December document.

STATE OF CONTESTED COUNTY ELECTIONS IN SCOTLAND   COUNTIES OF :

Mr. Solliciter General Dundass opposes the present member, Sir Alexander Gilmour, and must carry it, having nearly two to one of the old roll of freeholders, and he will have a considerable majority on the new roll when it shall

(1)
Edinburgh or Mid Lothian

---

[1] An obvious mistake by the compiler of the list ; Robinson was never Secretary to the Admiralty. This mistake is evidence tending to show that Robinson did not himself compile this list.

COUNTIES OF

(2)
Linlithgow or West Lothian

be made up. Sir William Cunningham, it is supposed, will have the support of the Earl of Hoptoun at next election, and whoever has his Lordship's interest will carry this county against the present member, Mr. Dundass, or anybody else.

(3)
Haddington or East Lothian

Mr. Nisbet of Dirleton, junior, and the Honourable Captain Stewart of the Guards, brother to Lord Blantyre, have declared themselves candidates for this county. If the latter joyns his interest to Mr. Nesbit's, it is thought this last will beat Sir George Suttie, the present member.

(4)
Lanerk

The two candidates are Mr. Campbell of Spanfield and Mr. Andrew Stewart. The latter will probably carry it as he has all the Hamilton interest besides numbers of Captain Lockhart Ross, (the present member), his connections.

(5)
Dumfries

Major Laurie, (son of Sir Robert Laurie), is a candidate for this county in the room of General Douglass, the present member, who is desirous to retire from parliament. The Major is supported by the Duke of Queensbury, whose interest in that county is greatly superior to everything that can be brought in opposition to it, though Mr Ferguson of Craigdarrock, (whose father was protected and supported by the Queensbury family), has vainly declared himself a candidate and is supported by Sir James Johnstone, Governor Johnstone's eldest brother.

(6)
Kirkudbright

Mr. Herron of Herron and Mr Stewart of Castle Stewart have declared themselves candidates in room of the present member, Mr. Murray of Broughton, who desires to retire from parliament. It is thought that whichever of the two candidates has the support of government, he will carry the election, as the numbers will run very near.

(7)
Ayr

Sir Adam Ferguson opposes the Honourable Mr. Kennedy, the present member for that county, and great numbers of new votes are made on both sides, but it is thought Mr Kennedy will in the end carry his election.

(8)
Renfrew

Mr. John Crawford is candidate in room of Mr. Macdowal, the present member, who retires from parliament. It is thought Mr. Crawford will certainly carry it, though he is opposed by Mr. Shaw Stewart, whose interest is very considerable in the county, but will hardly be able to stand in competition with the combined interests of Mr. Crawford, Mr. Baron Mure, and Mr. Macdowal.

Sir James Campbell of Adkindlass, who with his predecessors represented this county for many years till the last general election, has declared himself a candidate for it against Sir Lawrence Dundass's son, the present member. A great number of new votes have been made on both sides, and the contest will probably run very near.

(9) Sterling

In June, 1773, when Colonel Murray, (one of the present candidates), was chosen for the county, his brother, the Duke of Atholl, finding that even with all the efforts of government in his favor, the first question, (on which the election depended), was only carried by two votes, resolved to set his opponents at defiance by making such a number of new votes against the next general election as should ever after secure the county to his family. This measure gave an alarm to several of the most considerable gentlemen in it, who, in their turn, also set about creating votes to counterballance those of the Atholl family. Should therefore the whole new votes on both sides be found good ones, Mr. Graham of Balgowan, the other candidate, will, it is thought, have a majority of these in his favor.

(10) Perth

It is said that Sir Lawrence Dundass has been endeavouring to raise an opposition against the Duke of Argyle's interest in this county by setting up for it Captain Elphinstone, (Lord Elphinstone's second son), against Sir Archibald Edmondstone, the present member, but it is not thought that attempt will be attended with success.

(11) Dunbarton

Lord Adam Gordon, (invited by a majority of this county, where he has no fortune, to stand for it in room of Colonel Hepburn, General Graeme's brother-in-law, the present member), is the only candidate for it.

(12) Kincardine

General Fraser, the present member, is opposed by Lord George Gordon, the Duke of Gordon's third brother. Many new votes have been made by the Duke of Gordon for his brother and some by Sir Alexander Macdonald in favor of the General, but what may be the issue at the next election is difficult to determine, as there are several intricate circumstances attending this affair.

(13) Inverness

COUNTIES OF

(14)
Bamff

Lord Fife, the present member, is opposed by the Gordon family for some one of their friends. This contest will probably run very near in the end

(15)
Elgin

General Grant, the present member, is opposed by Mr Arthur Duff, brother to Lord Fife. This contest will also run very near, and it is probable that Colonel Munro and Sir Robert Gordon, who have not as yet declared for either side, may determine the fate of this election, Colonel Munro having *four* votes belonging to him, and Sir Robert *two.*

(16)
Clackmanan

Contested between Captain Erskine, (a grandson of the late Earl of Mar), and Colonel Abercrombie The former has an old family interest, and the latter is supported by Sir Lawrence Dundass. It is thought Captain Erskine will carry it.

The date of the following incomplete memoranda cannot be determined exactly, but they were prepared in the months just preceding the election of 1774. The transcript is marked " copied in full," so the remainder of the document is apparently not preserved among Robinson's papers

MINUTES AS TO ENGLAND.

[Seats, Etc.]	[Members Parliament 1768-74]	
Bedfordshire	Lord Ossory	See Lord Ossory, Lord Lieutenant
	Mr. Ongley	*The same* ; speak to the Dutchess of Bedford, Lord Gower, and Mr. Rigby thereon and see Lord Ossory and Mr. Ongley.
Bedford Town	*Mr. Vernon*	Doubtful whether again. Loss against.
Burgesses, free-men at large, in-habitants, house-holders.	*Mr. Whitbread*	See the same persons.
		See the Duke of St. Albans, Lord Lieutenant.
Berkshire	Mr. Vansittart	Same again ; see him.
	Mr Elwes	Query.

[Seats, Etc.]	[Members Parliament 1768–74]	
Reading .	Mr. Dodd . . .	Same again ; see him.
Freeman at large, inhabitants paying scot and lot.	Mr. H[enry] Vansittart.	Dead [1]
Abingdon . .	Mr N[athaniel] Bayley	A contest , see Mr. Morton on it.
Inhabitants paying scot and lot		
Windsor	*Mr. Keppell . . .*	Query, A contest against both. N.B.
By the last resolution in the corporation, but an old resolution in 1680 in inhabitants scot and lot	*Honourable Mr Montague*	Right of election ; may carry both ; see the Duke of *St. Albans*
Wallingford . .	*Mr. Aubrey . .*	Query.
	Mr. Cator . . .	Same again. See Mr. Justice Blakiston hereon. Query, If Colonel Pigot will stand again. If so, bring about an union between him and Cator. See Lord Pigot and also see Cator.
Buckinghamshire	*Lord Verney*	Query. Mr. George Grenville. *See him* or some of his friends.
	Mr. Lowndes . .	Same again ; see him. See Lord Despencer, Lord Lieutenant
Buckingham Town	Mr. Henry Grenville	*Same again*
	Mr. James Grenville	*Same again.*
Aylesbury . .	Mr. Bacon .	They say the *same again*, but, Query, A Nabob or two, and being outbid, see them It is said Mr. Charles Lowndes will offer himself.
	Mr. Durrand	
Chipping Wycombe	Mr. Waller	Same again ; see Mr. Waller.
	Mr. Barré	
Great Marlow .	Mr. Clayton .	Query, Same again ; see them ; see Mr. Cloberry.
	Mr. Dickinson	
Wendover .	Mr. E[dmund] Burke	Same again ; Mr. Scott says not, offers two ; is to bring a state of this borough
	Mr. Joseph Bullock	
Agmondesham	Mr. Drake, senior .	*Same again* ; see them.
	Mr. Drake, junior	
Cambridgeshire .	Sir J[ohn] Hynde Cotton	*Same again* ; see them.
	Sir S[ampson] Gideon	

---

[1] Henry Vansittart, formerly Governor of Bengal, a Director of the East India Company, touched at Cape of Good Hope on his way back to India in 1769 and was never heard of thereafter.

[Seats, Etc.]	[Members Parliament 1768–74]	
Cambridge University	Mr. Thomas Townshend, senior	Mr. Townshend declines; Lord Granby offers. Query, See the Duke of Grafton on it.
	Mr. Croftes	
Cambridge Town.	Mr. Cadogan . .	See Lord Montford and Mr. Cadogan and Mr. Jenyns. *Same again.*
	Mr. S[oame] Jenyns	
Cheshire . .	Mr. Egerton . .	See Lord Cholmondeley, Lord Lieutenant.
	Mr. Crewe . . .	*Same again if Mr.* Egerton will stand ; see him.
Chester .	Mr. Grosvenor .	*Same again ;* see them
	Mr. Bootle	
Cornewall .	Sir J[ohn] Molesworth	Lord Edgecumbe, Lord Lieutenant. Said to be a contest. See them, or Sir William *Lemon.*
	H[umphry] M[ackworth] Praed	
Launceston . .	Mr. Morrice . . .	A contest by Mr. John Buller.
	Mr. Amherst .	See Mr. Morrice.
Liskeard . . .	Mr. Elliot .	*Same again.*
	Mr. Salt	Query. See Mr. Elliot.
Lostwithiel .	Mr. H[enry] Cavendish	Query. See Lord Edgecumbe.
	Charles Brett	
Truro .	Hon. George Boscawen	*Same again.* See Lord Falmouth.
	Edward Hugh Boscawen	
Bodmin .	George Hunt . .	Said to be a contest. Mr. H. Dagge and Sir Christopher Triese. See Alderman of Bodmin. Mr. Hunt may bring in himself. Mr. Laroche says that he is secure. Speak to Lord F[almouth] and Lord Edgecumbe about it, but they have little interest.
	James Laroche	
Helston .	General Evelyn .	See Lord Godolphin. New charter. Query.
	Lord Clanbrassill .	P[eregrine] Cust must be one.
Saltash . . .	Mr. Hawke . . .	Query.
	Mr. Bradshaw .	Same again
East Looe .	John Buller . .	Same again
	John Purling . .	*Vacancy.* Speak to Mr. Buller on this, *and* settle with him.
West Looe .	James Townsend .	Two vacancies ; speak to Lord Chancellor and Mr. John Buller hereon.
	William Graves	
Grampound .	Grey Cooper . .	Two vacancies ; see Mr. Elliot on this ; venal.
	Charles Wolfran Cornwall	

[*Seats, Etc.*]	[*Members Parliament 1768–74*]	
Camelford .	Charles Philips . .	*One vacancy*, at least, if *not two.*
	William Wilson	See Mr. Philps hereon.
Penryn .	Hugh Pigot	Query, If not two vacancies. Sir
	Sir William Lemon	William Lemon will stand for the county of Cornewall. Lord Edgecumbe, see on this, who has an interest ; Mr. Bassett, Mrs Hearne, and friends ; independant , Baker Tredwen Etc
Tregony .	. Thomas Pownall .	See Lord Falmouth thereon. Mr
	Honourable John Grey	Symonds, who married the widow of Mr. Trevannion and is in possession of the family estates there has also a considerable interest, but the voters are [a] very venal sett.
Bossiney . .	Lord Mount Stuart	Same again.
	Sir George Osborne	Lady Bute and Lord Edgecumbe join to recommend one and one. See Lord Edgecumbe for *his* nomination.
St. Ives .	Adam Drummond .	Perhaps the same again, as the Duke of Bolton is for this time to recommend *one.*
	Thomas Durant . .	Vacant ; at Lord North's disposal 125 ; see *Mr, Praed.* His son, if a tenable place, if *not* another. If not a tenable place, another.
Fowey	. Mr. Rashleigh . .	Probably same again.
	Mr. M[odyford] Heywood	See Lord Edgecumbe. He and Mr. Rashleigh

1774, October 5.—Islip [1] Lord North to John Robinson   " I was detained at Bushy this morning. Let Pownall come in at Lostwithiel, and Conway at Tregony My noble friend [Lord Falmouth] is rather shabby in desiring guineas instead of pounds. . . . If he persists I would not have the bargain go off upon so slight a difference. I am afraid that it is too late for Kennett to succeed at Windsor as I have given the D[uke] of St. Albans leave to engage himself to Mr. Montague which he did on Monday, at

[1] This letter and some of the others that follow in this volume were printed in part in the Calendar of Robinson's papers published in the *Tenth Report of the Historical Manuscripts Commission*, Appendix, Part VI. With one or two exceptions, none of the letters therein printed are included in this volume unless the transcript contained matter not in the Calendar.

least he intended so to do after having learnt that I did not intend
to set up any opposition against him. That notion, I am afraid,
will have so much prevailed at Windsor that many of our friends
must be engaged. What interest we can yet give him is at his
service, but great care must be taken to explain to Mr. Neville
and Col. Philips that Kennett is not sent down by us, but has
undertaken the business on his own bottom. I am afraid that we
have lost a seat there by not setting up a candidate ourselves. . . .
I have [1] not had a narrow escape, but my postilion had. I lost
a very few guineas. I have promised Mr. Graves that he shall
come in for East Looe, as soon as we can place Sir Charles Whitworth in any other seat. The only persons I have still upon my
hands that are very pressing are Mr. Gascoign, Mr. Best, and Mr.
Irby for whom Lord Boston will pay 2000*l.* We have a chance
of Midhurst, of one seat at West Looe, and if Sir Abraham Hume
should be chosen for the Borough, of one seat at Petersfield. A
letter should be written to Joliffe in my name to secure the rever-
sion of Sir Abraham's seat."

1774, October 6.—Islip. Lord North to John Robinson. "I
am heartily sorry that we cannot settle the Welsh dispute. You
know that the seat at Plympton is at 3[000]. Lord H[oo]d should
be informed of that, as he said his son should pay 25[00] but that
I leave to your discretion, as well as the whole arrangement and
shall make but one or two observations upon it. Mr. Legge can
afford only 400*l.* If he comes in for Lostwithiel he will cost the
public 2000 guineas. I promised Mr. Butler that if we could find
a seat for Sir Charles Whitworth even before the Election, Mr.
Graves should come in for East Looe

"I think Gascoign should have the refusal of Tregony if he will
pay 1000*l.*, but I do not see why we should bring him in cheaper
than any other servant of the Crown. If he will not pay that
price he must give way to Mr. Best, if the latter will pay the money
required ; if he will not, but offers 2000*l.*, he may come in ; but
if he refuses to pay that sum I would have the seat offered to Mr.
Peachy.

"The arrangement then will stand thus :

| Minehead | . | . | Mr. Pownall. |
| Plympton | . | . | Mr. Conway and Lord Fairford. |

---

[1] Lord North had been attacked by a highwayman a few days previous,
and Robinson had written to congratulate him on his escape.

Lostwithiel . .	Mr. Legge or Sir Charles Whitworth.	
East Looe	Sir Charles Whitworth or Mr. Graves	
Tregony . .	General Parker and Mr. Gascoign, or Mr. Best, or Mr. Peachy.	

" I shall be satisfied with this arrangement in whatever way it is settled. The shortness of time will oblige you to take upon yourself to decide most of these smaller matters, and you may be certain, that I shall be satisfied with your decisions.

" As the Duke of Newcastle has come into our proposal, we must strain every nerve for his service. Mr. Sayer, Mr. Palmer, Capt. Fah, and every active man should be set to work immediately. By the success at the Poll for Mayor I have no great hopes of London, but it must not be neglected. Harley must come up immediately to scratch for Bull, or Wilkes will be sure for the Mayoralty.

" The whole list inclosed ought to have excuses written except Mr. Graves, with whom matters are settled, and Mr. Best or Mr. Peachy in case either of them should come in for Tregony. Tell Gascoign that if we can bring in Jenkinson for less than 1000l. we will not require so much of him. He had better venture, as we are much disposed to serve him.

" Sir Charles Farnaby had not been at Hithe on Monday morning, and many of the gentlemen talked of bringing in Sawbridge if he failed in the City. Even if he should succeed at Hithe, I do not believe that his friends would take another person at his recommendation, should he make his election for the City. But Sir Charles's inactivity will be very prejudicial, at least, I am afraid it will. Adieu : Dear Robinson, Yours most sincerely. North.

" P.S. I desire to be understood. I like your arrangement extremely and would have [you] determine immediately upon the receipt of this letter, without asking my opinion any more. I do not think that my promise to Mr. Graves will be at all broken by your arrangement, as Mr. Gascoign and Mr. Best have certainly a degree of claim upon me. The observations I made I only threw out for your consideration. Decide without delay. By my conversation with Sir James Peachy, I have reason to believe that he will pay the whole demand for his son, if we can serve him. N.

" P.S. Mr Best lives at *Chilston near Maidstone.* A messenger will quickly find him. You must desire a positive answer, for our affairs will not bear delay. Write in my name to Mr. Luttrell to recommend Mr. Pownall. Excuse me on account of my absence."

1774, November 19 —Downing Street. Lord North to John Robinson. " Everything in England goes on as well as we could expect. The state of America is neither better nor worse than when you were in London. I do not find my spirits flag, and am far from despairing of the republick. Let Cooper know whether you promised Masterman 2,500*l.* or 3,000*l* for each of Lord Edgcumbe's seats I was going to pay him 12,500*l.*, but he demanded 15,000*l.* and said that he had so settled it with you. Be so good also as to let me know by Cooper where my Red Book of Accounts with his Majesty is to be found, and if you have with you the key to the drawer or chest where it is kept, send it up by him. I want to know whether anything is due to me this quarter, and how much I may venture to take."

1775, September 6.—Hinchingbrook. The Earl of Sandwich to John Robinson. " My younger son's case is quite desperate When a vacancy happens at Huntingdon, I could wish to have a candidate ready to start immediately. I should not like a merchant or a meer moneyed man, for reasons which I have allready told you, and yet a sum of money will be necessary, tho' upon such terms as no one would refuse. The terms in short that I must have are 2,000*l.* to be lent to me for five years on my bond, and to pay the expenses of the election, which in all probability would not amount to 300*l.*

" I think there are many people in the world who would gladly accept these conditions ; while I am now writing one occurs to me, namely, Lord Carmarthen ; but I now write only for your opinion, and to desire as a friend that you would suggest to me one or more persons who you think would come up to my description, and who would be agreeable to Lord North ; I cannot as yet authorize you to make the proposal to any one for reasons I am going to mention to you, and I write merely that I may not be unprepared, and have more than one string to my bow.

" Mr. Banks who is now with Captain Phipps in Yorkshire, has sounded him about coming into Parliament through my means. I think he is not unlikely to accept my proposals, and I have now. written to tell him the conditions on which alone I can take him by the hand, namely, the *thinking and acting as I do in all American points and supporting the present administration in their whole system.*

I know his connection with opposition is entirely at an end, and that he wants much to come into Parliament ; therefore my opinion is that he will accept my offer, and if he does I think he will be a very good acquisition to us in the House of Commons. A week longer will bring this affair to a decision between Phipps and me, and by that time I shall have heard fully from you in answer to this letter."

1775, September 10.— —— The Earl of Sandwich to John Robinson   " I wish it may suit your convenience to be in town and that I may see you on Wednesday morning.   I shall before that time have heard from Captain Phipps, and be prepared to talk to you about the vacancy that I fear is too sure of happening at Huntingdon."

1779, July 12.— —— Charles Jenkinson to John Robinson. Recommends that a small pension be given to Abbé Jeaurinvilliers, as it is important to engage the writers of foreign gazettes.   Encloses :

(A) Letter from G Cressener to Charles Jenkinson, dated at Spa, July 4, 1779.   " The Abbé Jeaurinvilliers, ex-Jesuit, who writes the Cologne Gazette, has had a quarrel with the Chevalier d'Othée, who has the privilege of that Gazette from the Court of Vienna.   A pension of 600 livres a year for his life will keep him in our service   I have no view but the King's Service, the sum required is very small, the good resulting from it may be great. If I am well informed, the Writer of the Leyden Gazette hath a much larger Pension from the Opposition.   I shall only add on this Head, that I beg you would be so good as to mention this to your Friends in the Administration." [1]

[1] This letter is printed here because Mr. Stevens transcribed an interesting addition to the part of it printed in the Calendar of the Historical Manuscripts Commission.   This seems as good place as any for it in a collection of papers with which it has no other connection than the fact that it was sent to Robinson.

THE PARLIAMENTARY ELECTION
OF 1780

SECTION II

THE PARLIAMENTARY ELECTION OF 1780

1779, September 17.—Memorandum endorsement by John Robinson. "Covers in which the 24 Bank Notes of 500*l*. each were enclosed with his Majesty's Docquet thereon, and which were delivered by his Majesty to Lord North this day and given by Lord North to J[ohn] R[obinson] and which were sent to Mr. Drummond by me on the 18th and placed to the credit of my private account B——, and which sum was for twelve months of the additional 1,000*l*. per month from July, 1778, to June, 1779, inclusive "[1]

On the reverse side of this paper are the numbers of the notes, as follows : "No. K 613 ; 614 ; 205 ; 206 ; 624 ; 625 ; 214 ; 215 ; 532 ; 533 ; 534 ; 39. 12 notes of 500 each, 6,000*l*."

1779, September 18.—London. Receipt given to John Robinson by Andrew B. Drummond for Messrs. Robert and Henry Drummond and Company for " Twelve thousand pounds to account for on demand," described as " Enclosed in a sealed wrapper on which is written : Mr. Drummond's receipt for 12,000*l*. on account B——."

1780, August 13.—Bushy Park Lord North to John Robinson. " Private." " I have made it a rule this summer to allow myself no pleasure, nor dissipation, nor vacation whatever. . . . Provided the Parliament is to be dissolved (which it must now be, although the manner in which it will affect the militia seems to render it much more eligible to dissolve it in winter), it is and always has been indifferent to me when the dissolution shall [take] place. I only wanted to know from you the state of our affairs and your opinion of the proper moment. As to seeing Mr. Elliot, I always told you that it did not appear to me likely to be of any service ;

---

[1] For additional information concerning this fund see *infra*, pp. 143–146.

if he would serve us at all he would in his conversation with you have given you reason to expect it. I know nothing of the state of my promises as to Custom House Offices, but I cannot venture to engage a King's Patent Waiter's place to Dr. Williams. As to the 400*l.*, if you can let him have it I have no objection to it. He will not find us ungrateful for any successful negociation he may have with Mr. Elliot ; he never has found us so, and need not doubt of us. Employ him on that commission ; he is much more likely to succeed than I should be   I will write to Lord Edgcumbe, but, as I cannot promise him what he wants, my letter will I fear do more harm than good   The Lord Chancellor, to whom I gave last year constantly all my India papers and propositions, has constantly returned them to me at a great distance of time, without any opinion or assistance at all.   He has never mentioned to me the least anxiety upon that business this year, but has chosen to begin with it in the Closet for obvious reasons. In short, I see every day more and more the very disgraceful footing on which I am likely to continue while [I] remain in office, which, God knows, I have other causes enough to wish to quit.   I shall never do anything with the Duke of Newcastle by conversation or letter, but I will either write to him or call upon him to-morrow. He must certainly not see the Duke of Northumberland's letter.   If Mr. Fox stands, we shall have much trouble and more expense, which will all fall upon us.   Neither Lincoln nor Rodney will contribute."

1780, August 14—Syon Hill   John Robinson to Lord North. " Most private." " I do not think it at all necessary that you should deprive yourself of all relaxation.   On the contrary, I would recommend that you should have it publicly given out that you were gone to Kent for three weeks or a month   Parliament should be prorogued until the 31st of October or the 2nd of November. In the former case the Council should be held on the 31st of August or the 1st of September, and the proclamation and writs issued on the 1st or 2nd of September.   You might stay in Kent until the 28th of August, and return to Bushy on that day, unknown and unexpectedly, for while you and the ministers are still in and about town, a momentary dissolution is expected.   Before your going to Kent I trust to receive all your orders now necessary

" The Duke of Newcastle has wrote to Lord Lincoln to prevail on him to stand for Westminster, but your Lordship is perfectly right, it must be all at your expence.   However in that case it may be as well to fight for both as for one only, and the expence, after the *declaration*, which should be I think a day or two before the dissolution, will be equal only for two, as in a contest for one although the trouble will be more, probably. Sir Patrick Crauford has had the luck to stumble on Arundel, fortunately I believe for himself, if he will be content with that, but not so if [he] attempts another. It is unfortunate however for Lord Onslow, for his son Edward was to have come in there, but I told his Lordship a month ago that it would not do without money. He trusted in a junction of interest with Lord Surry, but told me that he would inquire about it, and it has now escaped his Lordship—for I yesterday heard through another channel that some other of the leaders were on Thursday last treating with another party for the seat and had agreed, but while together received the news that Sir Patrick had broke the ground, opened all the houses in town and come to terms with the people, therefore our other friend was too late and Sir Patrick for himself secure. I will however write to Sir Patrick and say to him that if he can secure the 2nd seat *undoubtedly*, a friend is ready to give 3,000*l*., and that he may be assured that friend will be agreeable to the people of Arundel, but that I doubt he will find that *they must* give Lord Surrey one member "

1780, August 21 —Windsor Castle. The King to John Robinson "Mr. Robinson, as the Dissolution is now fixed for Wednesday, August 30th, I think it right to transmit the money to you which compleats up to this month the 1000*l*. per month I have laid by. The other payments were made to Lord North himself ; I have wrote him word that I have sent it to you. I trust notice will be sent to the Chancellor for his appearance on that day at St. James's that no delay may arise in issuing the new writs."

[P.S.] " The amount of the notes is 14,000*l*."

1780, August 21.—Paper endorsed by John Robinson : " List of the Bank Notes received by me from his Majesty for 14,000*l* the 21st day of August, 1780, and sent by me to Messrs. Drummond on Account B—— the 22nd of August, 1780." The notes are listed indicating the denomination, the date, the number, and by whom signed.

1780, August 2.[1]—London. Receipt given to John Robinson by

---

[1] Despite the fact that the date appears as August 2 in two places on this document, it is probably a mistake for August 22. See the King's letter to Robinson on August 21 (above).

George Drummond for Messrs. Robert and Henry Drummond and Company for " Fourteen thousand pounds on account B—— to account for on demand." Endorsed on sealed wrapper, " 2d August, 1780. Mr. Drummond's receipt for 14,000*l*." [1]

1780, August 22.—Syon Hill, 10 A.M. Endorsed " Draft of note to His Majesty." " Mr. Robinson has the honour to acknowledge the receipt of your Majesty's commands of yesterday, with bank notes for 14,000*l*., which Mr. Robinson will take care to state to Lord North when Mr. Robinson sees his Lordship this morning, which he expects momentarily. The account of the distribution of this private fund shall be made up and transmitted to your Majesty.

" Mr. Robinson sent to Lord North on Sunday some Irish letters and a state of the manner of the dissolution of Parliament in 1774, and apprehends Lord North has transmitted these papers to your Majesty and submitted whether the like mode should not be pursued ; viz. : the Council held and Proclamation issued on Friday the 1st of September next, and the writs issue the 2d , returnable on Tuesday, the 31st of October.

" Mr. Robinson had the honour of a conversation of some hours with the Lord Chancellor the day he left town for Bath. It was then settled that he would come up to the Council for dissolving the Parliament. Mr. Robinson has been in a course of correspondence with his Lordship since, and will take care to apprize him when the day is fixed "

1780, September 5.—Hartelbury. The Bishop of Worcester to his brother, Lord North. . . . " The Corporation have sent two of their body privately to me wishing that a friend of mine should stand. Their account of the matter is, that the Corporation have never yet been beaten, that they are stronger now than they ever have been, as the Quakers are with them, that they have the assistance of all the Country Gentlemen against the Knight, and that in short they are certain of success if I will procure them a candidate with 1,500*l*."

" Under these circumstances, if truly stated to me, as I believe they are, Mr. Poulter, an active young man, and now a little known in this country, might really be made useful to rescue this seat out ‐

---

[1] Robinson preserved and Mr. Stevens transcribed a list of all these bank-notes, indicating their denomination, date, number, and by whom signed, but it does not seem worth while to give space to that information here.

of disagreeable hands ; but neither he nor I can advance. But if you know any way by which this may be made easy to him, or in part even made easy, so as that he shall risk no more than 4 or 500, I know he will be willing to engage in it, and is much mine and consequently your friend."

1780, September 6.—Receipt of Henry Drummond for " Robert Drummond, Self and Company " to John Robinson for " four thousand pounds on account B. to account for on demand." Accompanied by a half sheet used as a wrapper for bank notes Number A 656 and 657, 2,000*l* each payable to bearer and endorsed by Robinson " James Macpherson, Esquire, for his seat at Camelford. Paid to Mr. H. Drummond on Account B."

1780, September 6.—Receipt of Henry Drummond for " Robert Drummond, Self and Company " to John Robinson for " Four thousand pounds on Account B. to account for on demand." With this receipt was a wrapper endorsed by Robinson : " In this paper were four notes of 1,000*l*. each, total 4,000*l*., received of Mr. Pardoe for his son's seat at Camelford and were paid over to Mr. Drummond as per his receipt.".

1780, September 7.—Wroxton. Lord North to John Robinson. " I am sorry for Mr. Brudenell's peerage, which will make him and me ridiculous, and is the cause of Lord Talbot's, and will be the cause of Mr. Thynne's. . . . Mr. Langlois's dissatisfaction at his appointment is most unreasonable. . . . I have sent Mr. Duffell to Banbury to find out the five Gloucester votes, and I have given him authority to pay their expences to the poll. It would have been rather more convenient if Mr. Lloyd has informed you of the day of election in that city, but perhaps he may not know it himself. . . . Some people from the corporation of Worcester have been with the Bishop and have desired him to recommend a candidate whose success they will insure for 1,500*l*. Mr. Poulter, who has just married a sister of Mrs. North, would undertake it if he would be assisted as far as 1,000*l*. I have encouraged him with the promise that we would repay him 1,000*l*. if he would offer himself. He is now at Cambridge in the interest of Lord Hyde and Mr. Mansfield, and I hope he will not leave it till he has given his vote. I tell you this that you may be apprized of any thing I do concerning elections, and not be perplexed by any measure of mine. I shall avoid all other steps of this kind, but I left you in such despair about a candidate for Worcester, that I thought the Bishop's proposal ought not to be slighted. . . . By Eden's letter I perceive that he is extremely angry, but you see that the King is angry on the other side. What am I to do ? " [1]

1780, December 7.—Receipt of Robert Drummond for "Self, Henry Drummond, and Company" for "thirty thousand pounds to account for on demand." Endorsed by Robinson : "Messrs. Drummond's receipt for 30,000*l.* on private Account B."

1780, December 7.—Paper endorsed by Robinson, "Copy of Lord North's Note given this day to Mr. Drummond's (*sic*) for 30,000*l.*"

" I promise to pay to Messrs. Henry and Robert Drummond or order the sum of thirty thousand pounds with interest at the rate of five pounds per centum per annum as witness my hand this the seventh day of December, 1780." Memorandum added : " The above mentioned sum of money being for His Majesty's use, this note was shewn to His Majesty, given by his order, and approved of. North."

1781, March 6.—John Robinson to the King. " Mr. Robinson has this moment had the honour to receive your Majesty's commands with 6,000*l.* which he will take care instantly to have placed to the proper account. Mr. Robinson feels concerned that it has not been in his power to have that account as yet made up according to his wishes from the demands on it which cannot yet be concluded, but humbly begs leave to assure your Majesty that he will not fail to do it soon, the delay resting much on his mind."

1781, March 6 (?).—Wrapper endorsed : " Bank notes twelve of 500*l.* each, 6,000*l.*" Contains list of twelve following numbers : " K, 25 ; 26 ; 113 ; 114 ; 115 ; 116 ; 35 ; 36 ; 37 ; 38 ; O, 68 ; B, 81."

1781, March 6.—Queen's House, 48 m. past 8 a.m. The King to John Robinson. " Mr. Robinson shewed his usual propriety in transmitting to me last night the list of the speakers in the debate as well as the division.

" I take this opportunity of sending 6,000*l.* to him to be placed to the same account as that sent on the 21st of August. I have given notice of it to Lord North."

---

[1] It is not possible to be certain from the evidence that is on the transcription that these excerpts from a longer letter are in the order in which they were written. Cf. *Tenth Report Historical Manuscripts Commission*, Appendix, Part VI., p. 36.

1781, April 13.—Bushy Park, Friday Evening. Lord North to John Robinson. Endorsed: "Received 13th near midnight, answered 14th"

"I understand Mr. John Craigie is very fit for his office, and that the resignation of Mr. John Drummond is complete, without reservation or any consideration whatsoever. Upon these conditions I consented to the request of Lord Advocate in favour of Mr. Craigie.

"I suppose we must comply with the requests of Lord S[heffield] and Mr. D[aubeny]   The expences of both were incurred without my privity, or any promise on my part, and I was certainly ignorant of any expensive mode of carrying on the business of C[oventr]y having been adopted, as I was not consulted upon the business, and the option was made not by me but by Lord S[heffield]. As to Mr. D[aubeny], he applied for 4,000l., but had no promise. I wish however to please both of them, and the difficulty lies in the means of doing it. Are you able to find it ? I suppose the following sums will do : Lord S[heffield] 2,000l., Mr. D[aubeny] 1,500, being 500 more than he asked for at first and making in all an aid from us of 4,500l., which with Election of 1774, 2,000l., and ditto 1780, 1,000l , makes in all 7,500l

"I really think we shall do very handsomely in giving this 3,500l., but perhaps Mr. D[aubeny] will not be satisfied, and it will be necessary to give him more. Try to do this business as cheaply as possible. You will find it difficult enough to raise even the lowest sum

"Mr. Powney stipulated at first only for 1,000l. He has, I believe, had 1,500l. or 2,000l. What does he want now ? I shall have no objection to talk with him on the subject, but really the demands on this occasion are exorbitant beyond the example of any former time."

1781, September 3.—Wroxton. Lord North to John Robinson.

. [1] "I wonder how any notions have come to you that I had altered these arrangements. Mr. Harley, indeed, wrote me a letter in which he says expressly that he cannot and will not continue the remittance of the money unless 500,000l. is reserved beyond the 250,000l. paid to him and Mr. Drummond. If he writes such a

---

[1] The first part of this letter was not transcribed It is identified as item 1384 in the Abergavenny MSS. See *Tenth Report Historical Manuscripts Commission*, Appendix, Part VI., p. 45.

letter to me after having consented to a reservation of 250,000*l.* in a conversation with you, he has used me in a manner that makes me very little inclined to treat with him upon any business again."

———————

The following paper is endorsed : " 7th December, 1781. Abstract of Supposed State for 12th December, 1781." It is apparently an estimate based on a detailed canvass made five days in advance of the vote on the motion of Sir James Lowther for putting an end to the American War. The Parliamentary History (XXII, 831) gives the numbers in the division as 220 against the proposal to 179 for it.

Number of pro's in town 221 ; number of pro's out of town 43, of which probably may be got 14, as every one has been sent to twice or thrice ; hopeful in town 14, of which probably may be got 7 ; hopeful not in town 17, of which may probably be got 7 ; may possibly divide 249.

Number of con's, suppose *every one* in town 207 ; add all the doubtful present 11 ; and also all the doubtful absent 15 ; in this case they may divide 233.

1781, December 17.—Parliament Street. Monday morning. [John] Halliday to John Robinson. " Mr. Halliday presents his respectful compliments to Mr. Robinson and begs to offer, for his opinion, the inclosed proposal, which at present strikes him (from the perfect knowledge he has of the various characters that interest themselves in the elections at Taunton) as most likely if managed with address to prevent any contest of consequence if an election for that place should shortly become necessary." [1]

1781, December 17.—Enclosure in the above letter from Halliday to Robinson. " It may be proposed by one of the members of T[aunton] to some of the principal manufacturers there ; to induce them to decline engaging in an opposition to the corporation, if an election should be occasioned by the death of the other member, that, to preserve the peace of the town, and thereby not only prevent the injury and interruption that will necessary [necessarily] happen ·

———

[1] John Roberts, Mr. Halliday's colleague in the House of Commons, chosen in the general election of 1780, died shortly after the date of this letter and was succeeded in March of the next year by Benjamin Hammett.

from a contested election to the newly established silk manufacture, but to encourage the further progress of that manufacture and the more extensive employment of the poor in the town. He would propose to give in premiums in the manner as shall be recommended by a majority of the master workmen in that branch already introduced, and also to promote the engaging in other branches of the silk manufacture the sum of —— and to be applied towards preserving the woolen manufacture now on its decline in the town in premiums in manner and in proportion as shall be recommended by a majority of the principal persons engaged in that manufacture.

[The writer suggests in the margin of the paper five hundred pounds as necessary for the silk manufacturers and three hundred pounds for the woolen manufacturers]

" If the above proposal should be approved of, the whole remaining expence will be (as 'tis apprehended that after the vacancy happens, it will not be proper to open any houses of entertainment) : To 250 poor persons who have now a right to vote at an election, 29s each, 525l. To a publick dinner after the election and a piece of plate to the mayor, about 105l., making a total of 1,430l

" N.B It has been usual to give to the poor voters after the election is over 1 guinea each and a piece of plate to the Mayor of about 15l. value.

" It must be observed that all the principal manufacturers of T[aunton] are Dissenters and much at enmity with the corporation, who will not admit any person of that description to become a magistrate of the town. An opposition to any candidate that the corporation approve is therefore mostly to be apprehended from them. It is proposed to prevent any effectual opposition by endeavouring to stop it at the fountain head in the manner here recommended, which 'tis believed will have that effect."

1781, December 27.—— —— Thomas Exon to John Robinson. . . .

" Mr. Halliday and myself request the honor of your immediate answer and whether we are authorized to proceed in execution of the scheme which will effectually prevent all the trouble and if Mr. Halliday shall advance the —— or draw on any banker you appoint ? I am this moment informed General [1] continues

[1] Perhaps John Roberts, member for Taunton at the time this letter was written, who died shortly thereafter and was succeeded by Benjamin Hammett March 20, 1782.

extremely ill. In consequence of your answer, Mr. Halliday and myself shall instantly proceed on our journey, as no time is to be lost, and our most ardent wish is to render effectual and essential service to government which a delay may partly prevent."

1782, January 18.—Paper endorsed by John Robinson : " Memorandum of bank notes sent to Messrs. Drummonds this day to be placed to the credit of my account B——, 2,400*l.* and also 310*l.* 17*s.* sent 22nd of February, 1782." The paper lists each note with its number, denomination, and date.

1782, February 15.— —— Lord North to John Robinson. . . . " I understand Governor Tryon's business better, and have still a doubt whether we can without the utmost danger of blame and of establishing a bad precedent, allow any part of the 3,000*l.* for the House. Weigh well the difficulty, and if it is not too great, send away the letter.

" I inclose a summoning letter sent to me by Sir Francis Bassett to give him the decisive answer I promised. I cannot give it him, but I have no right to expect him to remain undetermined, so that, I fear, I must let him take his course, the consequence of which will be the defection of himself and his three friends to the enemy. We can but ill spare them."

———

The following paper is endorsed : " 15 March, 1782. Remarks." On that date occurred the debate and division on the motion of Sir John Rous on the question of a lack of confidence in North's administration. The division is given by the Parliamentary History (XXII, 1199) as 227 yeas and 236 noes. A list of the members voting on both sides is given in the same publication

Persons with before who changed : Farrer ; Dunsdale ; Sir G. Elliot ; 3.

Persons who were hopeful, who now came and voted against : Child ; Wrottesley ; Fludyer ; Garden ; Nisbet ; 5.

Persons who were said not to go the whole length with them but who did vote with them as before : Hungerford ; Penruddock ; Rolle ; Knightley ; 4.

Persons who went away : Neville ; Trentham ; D'Oyley ; Dawes ; Sinclair ; 5.

Persons who staid away   Jackson ; Darker, ill ; Sir William Gordon, very ill , Lord Lincoln, would not come though his father wrote to him ; Lord William Gordon, can't now vote so *lost* ; Richard Middleton ; Mackworth ; A. Douglas, said to be in town but did not take his seat as Windham did ; Anthony Eyre, at Bath at Lord Lincoln's ; Noel Hill, staid away at request ; Gough ; 11, and I doubt not on going carefully through the whole list I shall find more.

New persons who did not vote before, that were now got up, and were with us : Anstruther ; Cecil ; Duntze , Durand ; Lord Adam Gordon ; Harley ; Harvey ; Hudson ; Jolliffe ; Lascelles ; Masterman ; Alexander Murray , Sollicitor General of Scotland ; Purling , Ross ; Ward ; J. York ; Gilbert ; Lord Hyde , Boscawen ; Methuen ; 20   These should have greatly increased our numbers.

New persons that opposition got up and voted against us : Barrington ; Goddard, who was said to be off with Vernon ; Luther, brought in, could not walk ; Sir George Savile ; Wilkes ; Wyndham, took his seat on purpose ; Gipps ; 7.

Pros that could not be got : E. Bacon ; Sir M. Burrell ; Burton and Davenport, circuit ; Sir J. Eden ; Lord R. Manners ; General Monckton ; Sir H. Owen ; 8.

Cons that could not be got : Sir P. Blake ; R. H. Coxe ; Dempster ; Noel ; Scudamore ; Wenman ; Woodley ; 7

1782, March 15.—The Admiralty. The Earl of Sandwich to John Robinson " I had rather defer settling our money business until Sunday or Monday morning when I shall be ready for you at any hour you will name. From what I have heard to-day I am persuaded that if Lord North did not despond and talk of giving the thing up, matters would not yet be irretrievable."

1782, March 19.—Admiralty. The Earl of Sandwich to John Robinson. " I wish much to see you and beg we may contrive to meet in the course of this day to settle our money business, which should not be delayed any longer. I saw a certain considerable person yesterday, who is much to be lamented. He is very firm and seems to be inclined to do everything that is dignified and judicious I afterwards saw Rigby who desponds totally and thinks that further reistance is in vain."

The Stevens transcripts include the following memorandum. Perhaps Robinson did not preserve a complete copy. If preserved, the original might be among the Landsdowne papers. The transcript is marked : " Copied in full." The King wrote to Robinson August 7, 1782 : " I cannot at the same time avoid expressing my approbation of his [Robinson] having undertaken to furnish Lord Shelburne with an accurate state of the House of Commons and the connections of each of them as far as can be ascertained. This will be very material to counteract the activity of Mr. Fox, who every honest man and those in the least interested in the support of the constitution must wish to do the utmost to keep him out of power."

1782, August 7.—Memorandum by John Robinson for Lord Shelburne endorsed, " State of Representation and Remarks," headed " Most Private."[1]

" Nothing can be more difficult than to form a state of the political sentiments of the House of Commons in the present Juncture. In a stable, permanent government to whom gentlemen have professed friendship, with whom they have in general acted, and from whom they have received favors, conjectures may be formed with a tolerable certainty of the opinions which gentlemen will entertain on particular questions, but in a state so rent as this has lately been, torn by intestine divisions, and split into different parties, with an administration to be established, after one has been overturned and another divided, it is the hardest task that can be to class them. The attempt to do it leads into so great a field and requires so large a discussion that it renders the business almost impossible. However, in obedience to your Lordship's commands the following state has been drawn out and is submitted, but it even must be subject to much discussion and explanation on every part of it to comprehend the minute and true state of each part and of individuals."

[1] *Tenth Report Historical Manuscripts Commission*, Appendix, Part VI., p. 53.

Pro.	Hopeful	Doubtful	Con.		
1				*Abingdon :* John Mayoi	Has strong personal interest and connections at Abingdon through which he brings himself in, and apprehends he can continue to do so. Has rendered services to the Revenue, and has expectations of office as a reward.
	1			*Agmondesham .* William Diake, Sr.	Their own Borough. Independent
	1			William Drake, Jun.	country gentlemen, desirous of peace, and friends to the constitution. Consequently may be expected to support administration in all such questions ; in others will probably fluctuate
			1	*St Albans* John Radcliffe	Mr. Radcliffe comes in partly on his
			1	William Charles Sloper	own interest, conjoined with Lord Spencer. Mr. Sloper entirely brought in by Lord Spencer. Both most probably will be against
1		1		*Aldborough, Suffolk :* Martyn Fonnereau P. C. Crespigny	Bring themselves in, and have the Borough ; [impossible ?] without great expence indeed to oppose them and then the success very doubtful. Were friends of the old administration. Mr. Crespigny had a favor from Lord North to his wife. Holds a nominal place, but *no salary.* Mr. Fonnereau is independant but well inclined to government.
1			1	*Aldborough, Yorkshire :* Mr. [Charles] Mellish Mr. Samuel Fludyer	The Duke of Newcastle's borough, and these gentlemen are brought in by him. Mr. Mellish is the son of Mr. William Mellish, Receiver General of the customs. He always acted with the Duke of Newcastle. Sir Samuel Fludyer is the nephew of Mr. George Brudenell. Sir Samuel was much the friend of Mr. Fox and acted with him.

Pro.	Hopeful.	Doubtful	Con.		
				Andover :	
1				Sir John Griffin	Brought in by themselves and their
1				Benjamin Lethieullier	own attention. They are two very independent gentlemen. Sir John Griffin was almost always in opposition to the old government, Mr. Lethieullier sometimes with it. Sir John may go with General Conway, and it is likely that Mr. Lethieullier will ; they are therefore set down as hopeful.
		1		*Anglesea :*	
				Lord Bulkeley	Comes in with the support of his friends but has a strong interest against him in Lord Paget and might be affected by government. He goes with his father-in-law, Sir George Warren, and was by him carried against the old administration on his disappointment, although not adversely inclined. He was a great personal friend of Lord Temple, but may be esteemed very doubtful.
			1	*Appleby :*	
1				Philip Honeywood	Mr. Honeywood is brought in by Lord Thanet and will go with him most likely. Much connected with the Cavendishes, etc., etc. Mr. Pitt through Sir James Lowther and in office.
				Hon. William Pitt	
1				*Arundel :*	
	1			Thomas Fitzherbert	These gentlemen are both brought in by *themselves.* The latter aided somewhat by Lord Surry. Mr. Fitzherbert has material connections with the Ordnance and should go with government. Mr. Baker may be reckoned, it is thought, hopeful with a little attention, as he was against the old administration mostly when he attended, but indeed that was not much.
				Peter William Baker	
	1			*Ashburton .*	
1			1	Charles Boone	Mr. Boone comes in on Lord Orford's
				Robert Palk	interest and is a very independent

Pro.	Hopeful	Doubtful	Con.		
					man. Was pretty closely attached to the old administration and in long habits of friendship with Mr Rigby, and his friends may be hopeful Mr Palk comes in through his own interest and connection and will be with.
1	1			*Aylesbury :* Anthony Bacon Thomas Orde	Brought in by themselves on Mr. Bacon's popular interest there. Mr. Bacon had connections with government, but they are all now put an end to, yet may be hopeful with attention. Mr. Orde in office.
	1			*Banbury :* Lord North	Comes in as a family borough.
	1		1	*Barnstaple :* John Cleveland Francis Bassett	Mr. Cleveland comes in by his own interest, aided by the government interest, but which is now very materially affected there by Mr. Crew's Bill. He has always been connected with government and generally supported them, though sometimes shy. However, it is thought that he may be reckoned hopeful at least with attention. Mr. Bassett came in on his own interest and his friends there. Is an independent country gentleman and was a friend of the old administration. Is connected with and most probably will go with his relation, Sir Francis Bassett; at present, therefore, must be classed doubtful.
1	1			*Bath :* Abel Moysey Hon. Mr. [John Jefferys] Pratt	Come in on the interest of their friends in that corporation. Mr. Moysey is well inclined to support administration; owed his office to Lord North, and may, it is thought, be classed hopeful. Mr. Pratt with.
		1		*Beaumaris :* Sir George Warren	Brought in by Lord Viscount Bulkeley, vide remark at Anglesea. It is thought must be classed doubtful.

Pro.	Hopeful.	Doubtful.	Con.		
			1	*Bedfordshire :*	
	1			Earl of Upper Ossory	Lord Ossory may perhaps not wrongly be classed Con. Mr. St. John perhaps may be hopeful.
				Hon. St. Andrew St. John	
1				*Bedford town :*	
				Sir William Wake	Come in on their own and their friends'
	1			Samuel Whitbread	interest there. Sir William Wake may be for. Mr. Whitbread less decided perhaps, and at present only hopeful.
	1			*Bedwin :* Sir Merrick Burrell	Brought in by Lord Aylesbury but
	1			Paul Cobb Methuen	act independently. Sir Merrick Burrell attends but little ; was a friend of the old administration and supported them ; with attention probably may be got, and therefore classed hopeful.
					Mr. Methuen attends but little also, when he did he mostly supported the old government. Is very independent, but may perhaps be classed as hopeful.
	1			*Beeralston :* Lord Fielding	These gentlemen come in under the
	1			Lawrence Cox	protection of the Duke of Northumberland. They both supported the old administration and with attention may probably continue, but at present can certainly be only at most reckoned hopeful.
1				*Berkshire :* John Elwes	Both these gentlemen opposed the old
			1	Winchcombe H. Hartley	administration. One of them will probably support this ; the other very likely take the Rockingham line.
	1			*Berwick :* Hon. Gen. [John] Vaughan	These gentlemen come in on their respective family interests there.
	1			Sir J. H. Delaval	They both supported the old government. General Vaughan will go with his brother, Lord Lisburn, who professes great attachment to the old government. Sir J[ohn] H[ussey] Delaval perhaps is also hopeful

Pro.	Hopeful.	Doubtful.	Con.		
					with attention, and therefore they are both classed so.
			1	*Beverly :* Sir James Pennyman, Bart	Come in on their own interests there. Are connected with the Rocking-
			1	Evelyn Anderson	hams and classed as such, against.
	1			*Bewdley :* Lord Westcote	Family interest. Connected much with the old administration but yet from all circumstances it is thought may properly be classed hopeful.
1	1			*Bishops Castle :* ' William Clive Henry Strachey	Come in under Lord Clive's protec- tion. Mr. Clive will certainly go as Lord Clive does, and may be classed as hopeful. Mr Strachey in office
1	1			*Bletchingly :* Sir Robert Clayton John Kenrick	Sir Robert Clayton was always against the old government and conse- quently may be thought will sup- port the present, but with him that is not a certain rule. It is ventured however to class him hope- ful. Mr. Kenrick is in office. The borough is a family one.
1	1			*Bodmyn :* George Hunt William Masterman	These two gentlemen come in on their own separate independent interests with the electors of this borough. Mr. Hunt always opposed the old administration, may therefore be hopeful to the present if his Rock- ingham connections do not over- ballance ; it is not known that they do, and therefore he is classed as hopeful. Mr. Masterman's per- sonal connections are with Lord Edgecumbe, but he has others also, and holds office under the Dutchy of Lancaster. He is therefore classed pro.
	1			*Boroughbridge :* Anthony Eyre	Come in under the protection of
	1			Charles Ambler .	the Duke of Newcastle, go with his Grace, and supported the old

Pro.	Hopeful	Doubtful	Con.		
					administration. May perhaps be classed hopeful.
				Bossiney .	
	1			Hon. H. L. Lutterell	The borough is between Lady Bute
	1			Hon. Charles Stuart	and Lord Edgecumbe These gentlemen both supported the old administration whenever they were present, and it is supposed may be classed hopeful to the present.
				Boston :	
	1			Sir Peter Burrell	Come in on their own, their families',
	1			Mr. [Humphry] Sibthorpe	and friends' interest in this place. They both were supporters of the late administration and friends to it. And it is thought with attention may be classed hopeful to the present.
				Brackley :	
	1			John William Egerton	Come in under the protection of the
	1			Timothy Caswell	Duke of Bridgwater and will go with his Grace and his friends. May therefore be hopeful.
				Bramber ·	
				Sir Henry Gough	Sir Henry Gough comes in on his own
				Capt. [Henry Fitzroy] Stanhope	interest as having at least half the borough and having compromised with the Duke of Rutland.
				Breconshire :	
		1		Charles Morgan	Independent. Desirous of peace, a friend to the constitution, a supporter of the old government in most cases. Had some family connections with the Cavendishes, yet may be hopeful. However, considering all circumstances, classed doubtful as safest.
1				*Brecon Town :*	
				Sir Charles Gould	Brought in by his brother-in-law, Mr. Morgans. In office
1 1	31	7	7 [1]		

1782, August 21.—Upper Harley Street. Thomas Orde to John Robinson. "Lord Shelburne desires to have the pleasure of seeing you at Wycombe on Saturday next to dinner at five o'clock, and hopes that you will stay Sunday. Respecting the seat I am to inform you in confidence that we are in treaty about one with Lord N——n [1] for Gatton. I almost venture to guess that it is the same which has engaged your attention. I do not ask to know your secret if it is improper. I perfectly trust in your friendly assistance to aid as much as possible. It really however seems to be a hard bargain, considering circumstances, and you know that we are not rich. He would surely take less, and we may then contrive to seat our Northern Friend before the meeting of Parliament."

1783, April 15.—Lord North to John Robinson. "Dear Robinson, I should [be] much obliged to you if you could procure from Mr. Harley or Mr. Drummond or some other of your friends some of the loan for one or both of the persons whose names are inclosed." Enclosure :

"London, 14th April, 1783. For Thomas Farrer of Mark Lane, ten thousand pounds. For John Ruse of Croydon, Surr[e]y, ten thousand pounds, subject to the conditions of the loan."

The following, from the transcript, apparently a first draft of a report to some interested person, is endorsed in pencil : " Query, Whether this should be copied for his Majesty. I think it shewed attention to reduce." The cases mentioned in the document are all in the last years of North's administration, one dating as late as 1782. It is probable, therefore, that the memorandum was prepared either in the course of the debate on economic reform just previous to or after the accession of Rockingham, though it is possible the paper dates after the accession of Pitt in 1783.

ACCOUNT OF PENSIONS EXTINGUISHED AND NOT RETURNED.

Peers.

Lord Say and Seele 600*l.* ; Earl of Peterboro 400*l.* ; Lord Willoughby of Parham 400*l.* ; Earl of Essex 900*l.* Query,

---

[1] Probably Lord Newhaven, a baron in the Irish peerage, who was himself one of the members for Gatton in this parliament. Robert Mayne, who was elected the second member in 1780, died about the time this letter was written.

Whether this should be retained This is supposed to be extinguished by the demolition of the place to which it was annexed. Query, Whether it is yet abolished [1] ; Lord Edgecumbe 800*l.* The place to which this was annexed is taken away from him and extinguishes it ; Total peers ceased 3,100*l.*

Members of Parliament

Mr. Harley, for several years on provision by contract, 1,000*l* ; Mr. Bull, ceased on his quitting parliament, 600*l.* ; Mr. Dodd, on his death, 750*l.* ; Mr Garth, on his quitting parliament and being provided for in the Excise, 500*l* ; Mr. Richard Whitworth, on ditto, his being out of parliament, 600*l.* ; Mr. Anthony Bacon on his having a contract, 600*l.* ; Captain Wolseley, on his being out of parliament, but returned afterwards and pension took place to repay him for expences and losses by his not going abroad to Munich Returned in the book. 600*l.* ; Colonel Carey, on his being out of parliament, 500*l* ; Mr Cruger, when out of parliament, 500*l* ; Mr. William Stuart, when he left parliament, 500*l.* ; Mr. Baldwyn, on his being out of parliament, 600*l* ; Mr. Johnes, on his having the Auditor of Wales, 500*l.* ; Mr. Macpherson, on the regulation made of it, 500*l* ; Total members ceased 7,750*l*

Other Pensions.

Count Gentile, on his death, 200*l.* ; Mr. G. L. Scott, on his death, 600*l* ; Mr. Lobiniere, on his leaving the country, 400*l.* ; Reverend Mr. Coryton, when provided for in the Church, 200*l.* ; Total 1,400*l.* ; Making a grand total of 12,250*l.*

The following list is undated, but was apparently prepared in the course of the struggle between the Coalition and their opponents in the last weeks of 1783, either just before or just after the accession of Pitt, probably just after The date is between November 19, 1783, and January 1, 1784.

---

[1] The explanatory statement referring to Lord Essex is drawn through in the transcript, apparently so in the original.

ENGLISH COUNTIES.

County.	Members.	Abroad.	Ill ; can't attend.	Pro.	Hopeful.	Doubtful	Con
Bedfordshire	Lord Ossory						1
	Andrew St. John . . .						1
Berkshire	John Elwes						1
	W. H. Hartley . . .						1
Bucks . .	Lord Verney						1
	Thomas Grenville . . .						1
Cambridge	Sir Henry Peyton . .			1			
	Philip Yorke . . .			1			
Cheshire . .	Robert John Crewe						1
	Sir Robert Cotton . .			1		-	
Cornwall . .	Sir William Lemon . .			1			
	Edward Elliot . . .			1			
Cumberland .	Sir James Lowther . .			1			
	Sir Henry Fletcher . .						1
Derbyshire	Nathanael Curzon. . .			1			
	Lord George Cavendish .						1
Devon. . . .	John Parker [1]	1			1		
	John Rolle. . . .			1			
Dorset . . .	Humphry Sturt . . .					1	
	George Pitt . . .				1		
Durham . .	Sir Thomas Clavering .		1				
	Sir John Edens .						1
Yorks	Henry Duncombe . .			1			
	Vacant [2]				1		
Essex	John Luther						1
	T. B. Bramston . . .			1			
Gloucester	James Dutton						1
	George Berkley . . .					1	
Hereford . .	Thomas Harley . .			1			
	Sir George Cornwall . .						1
Hertford . . .	William Plummer. .						1
	Thomas Halsey . . .					1	
Huntingdon	Lord Hinchinbrook . .						1
	Lord Ludlow . .						1
Kent	Charles Masham . . .			1			
	Filmer Honywood .			1			

[1] After the name of John Parker there is a score in ink in the "hopeful" column, and one in pencil in the column marked "abroad" There is also in faint pencil the statement, "will not attend."

[2] The name "Mr. Foljambe" appears in the transcript as erased, and the word "vacant" follows. The seat in question is left in the "hopeful" column Sir George Savile, long one of the members for Yorkshire, accepted the stewardship of East Hendred in the last weeks of 1783, his nephew Francis Foljambe, who succeeded him, serving from January 1, 1784, until the dissolution of parliament in March of that year.

ENGLISH COUNTIES—*continued*

County.	Members.	Abroad.	Ill; can't attend.	Pro.	Hopeful.	Doubtful.	Con.
Lancashire . .	Sir Thomas Egerton . .			1			
	Thomas Stanley . . .						1
Leicestershire	J. P. Hungerford .				1		
	William Pochin .			1			
Lincoln . . .	C. A. Pelham . . .						1
	Sir John Thorold . . .						1
Middlesex	George Byng						1
	John Wilkes			1			
Monmouthshire .	John Hanbury (abroad) .						1
	John Morgan					1	
Norfolk . . .	T. W. Coke . . .						1
	Sir Edward Astley . .			1			
Northampton .	Lucy Knightly . . .				1		
	Thomas Powis. . . .			1			
Northumberland.	Lord A. Percy . . .			1			
	Sir William Middleton .					1	
Nottingham .	Lord Edward Bentinck .						1
	Charles Meadows . . .					1	
Oxford . . .	Lord Wenman. . . .			1			
	Lord Charles Spencer .						1
Rutland .	Thomas Noel . . .		1				
	George B. Brudenell .			1			
Shropshire . .	Noel Hill			1			
	Sir Richard Hill . . .			1			
Somerset . .	R. H. Coxe . . .		1				
	Sir John Trevelyan . .			1			
Hampshire .	Jervoise Clarke . . .						1
	Robert Thistlewaite . .			1			
Stafford . . .	Sir John Wrottesley . .			1			
	Lord Lewisham . . .						1
Suffolk . . .	Sir Charles Bunbury . .						1
	Sir John Rous . . .			1			
Surrey . . .	Sir Joseph Mawbey . .			1			
	Sir Robert Clayton . .						1
Sussex . . .	Lord George Lenox . .			1			
	Thomas Pelham . . .						1
Warwick .	Sir R. Lawly . . .					1	
	Sir G. Shuckburgh . .			1			
Westmorland .	Sir M. Fleming . . .			1			
	James Lowther . . .			1			
Worcester	Edward Foley . .						1
	William Lygon . .					1	
Wiltshire . . .	Charles Penruddock . .				1		
	Ambrose Goddard .				1		
	Totals	1	3	32	7	8	30

WALES.

Constituency.	Member.	Abroad.	Ill ; can't attend.	Pro.	Hopeful.	Doubtful.	Con.
Anglesea . . .	Lord Bulkley . . .			1			
Beaumaris . .	Sir G. Warren.	1					
Brecon . .	Charles Morgan .				1		
Brecon Town .	Sir Charles Gould. .			1			
Cardiff . . .	Sir H. Mackworth .			1			
Cardiganshire .	Lord Lisburne . . .					1	
Cardigan . . .	John Campbell of Calder	1					
Carmarthenshire .	John Vaughan. . . .					1	
Carmarthen .	George Philips. . . .					1	
Caernarvonshire .	John Parry . . .			1			
Caernarvon . .	Glynn Winn . .			1			
Denbighshire .	Sir W. W. Wynn .			1			
Denbigh . . .	Richard Middleton . .				1		
Flintshire . . .	Sir Roger Mostyn. . .						1
Flint . .	Major Watkin Williams .			1			
Glamorganshire	Charles Edwin. . . .					1	
Haverfordwest .	Lord Kensington . . .				1		
Merionethshire .	Evan Lloyd Vaughan .					1	
Montgomeryshire	William Mostyn Owen .						1
Montgomery . .	Whitshed Keene . . .						1
Pembrokeshire .	Sir Hugh Owen . . .					1	
Pembroke . .	Mr. Hugh Owen . . .				1		
Radnorshire .	Thomas Johnes . . .			1			
Radnor .	Edward Lewis . . .			1			
	Totals		2	9	4	6	3

1783, December 22 —"Memorandum   H[enry] D[rummond] to
have Lord M[ountague]'s support and interest at M[idhurst] to be
returned for that Borough for the next parliament in case the
present parliament shall be dissolved on or before the 25th of
March next and to sit, if he lives, during the time and he chooses
it for that Borough for the whole of the next time as that parliament
shall continue parliament be it seven years or for a shorter, and if
Mr. D[rummond] chooses at any time during the next parliament
to vacate his seat and to be chose again, or to nominate another
friend to this seat in parliament, Mr. H[enry] D[rummond] is to
be at full liberty so to do for the residue of that parliament, and

Lord M[ountague] engages to give his support and interest to return Mr. H[enry] D[rummond] or his nominee again for the residue of the time the next parliament shall continue, but no longer, Mr H[enry] D[rummond] or his nominee for each such change or return after the first return in the next parliament paying the sum of 200*l.* for the expences of each such return and change.

Mr. H[enry] D[rummond] 3xxx—15th—D—post Re.

This to be no effect until Lord M[ountague] shall return to Cowdray, when he will by letter signify the same."

The date of the following is obviously between the accession of the Pitt administration in December, 1783, and the dissolution of parliament, March 25, 1784:

" In the several divisions upon the East India Bill and the Address there were 259 votes in all given for the late ministry according to their own list of them.   Of these, we now canvass 42 positively *pro,* which in our last canvass stood as following, viz., *Pro*: A. Bacon , L. Cox ; Lord F. Campbell , William Chaytor ; Sir J. Cockburn ; Major Campbell ; Mr. Curzon ; Mr. Caswall ; Sir E. Deering ; Sir A. Edmonstone ; Archibald Fraser ; Sir C. Gould ; Mr. Greville ; George Graham , Mr. Johnes ; Sir Thomas Laurie ; Mr. Masterman ; General Morris ; Mr. Murray , John Ord ; John Stevenson ; Gabriel Steward ; Mr. Sinclair ; Philip Stephens ; Total 24.

Hopeful : Mr. Blackwell ; Mr. Fludyer ; Mr. Hatton ; Mr C. Morgan ; Total 4.

Doubtful : Mr Amcotts ; Mr. Calvert ; Sir Henry Clinton ; Mr. Halliday ; Mr. Lloyd ; J. Morgan ; Total 6.

Con · Mr. Ambler ; Mr Cleveland ; Anthony Eyre ; Mr. Evelyn ; Sir Charles Farnaby , Sir Samuel Fludyer ; Lord Hinchinbroke ; Mr. Mellish ; Total 8 ; Grand total 42.

So that out of these names we gain to our former *pro's* as follows : 8 out of the *con's* ; 6 out of the doubtful ; 4 out of the hopeful, making 18, and the general recapitulation, so altered, would stand : 240 pro ; 57 hopeful ; 39 doubtful ; 196 con ; 26 absent ; 558 total."

" Besides what precedes, there are in the list of the 259 who voted 36 other members who are now thought very hopeful and which in the former canvass only stood as follows, viz.

Pro : Sir William Dolben ; Adam Drummond , Lord William Gordon ; Edward Lewis , John Purling ; George Rodney ; Total 6.
Hopeful : Mr. Burrard ; Mr. Bricklade ; Mr. Crespigny ; Mr. F. Cust ; Mr. Daubeny ; Mr. Ewer ; Mr. Fonnereau , Sir H Hoghton ; Mr. Hungerford ; General Murray ; Sir G. Osborne ; Mr Peachy ; Henry Rawlinson ; Total 13.
Doubtful : Mr. Bowes ; Lord Lisburn ; Sir James Marriot ; General Vaughan ; Total 4.
Con : Mr. Charteris ; Mr. Dickenson , Admiral Darby ; Mr. Davies ; Sir S. Gideon ; Sir H. Gough ; Mr. Hale ; Sir Robert Herries ; Mr. Jolliffe ; Mr. Poulett ; Mr. Rigby ; Mr. A. Rawlinson ; Mr. Sloane ; Total 13   In all 36." [1]

The documents immediately following relate to a fund which the king diverted from his privy purse for election expenses at the rate of one thousand pounds per month, beginning November, 1777, and ceasing on the resignation of North. The date of the first paper, which is endorsed " Most Private State," is apparently March, 1782.

" Memorandum · The additional 1,000*l.* a month to his Majesty's Privy Purse commenced for the month of November, 1777.

		l.	*s.*	*d.*
1778				
January	His Majesty paid Lord North for the months of November and December, 1777 . . .	2,000	0	0
6 February	Received for January and February . . .	2,000	0	0
26 June	Received for 4 months, March, April, May,		0	0
	and June . . ِ	4,000	0	0
1779				
17 September	Received for 12 months from July, 1778, to June, 1779, inclusive	12,000	0	0
1780				
21 August :	Received for 14 months from July, 1779, to August, 1780, inclusive	14,000	0	0

[1] This paper is placed here rather than in its proper chronological place because all of the papers that follow in this section relate to another subject, namely, the money diverted by the king from his privy purse for election purposes.

			l.	*s.*	*d.*
1781					
6 March	Received for 6 months from September, 1780, to February, 1781, inclusive		6,000	0	0
	Total received from his Majesty .		40,000	0	0
	Received by Lord North otherwise as contributions towards the expenses of the several elections		30,010	17	0
	Total received		70,010	17	0
	Disbursed as by the general account . . .		103,765	15	2
	Deduct receipts as above		70,010	17	0
	Ballance due to Lord North . .		33,754	18	2

" For which expences Lord North, on the 7th of December, 1780, borrowed of Messrs. Drummond 30,000*l.* and by his Majesty's orders gave to Messrs Drummond a promissory note for that sum. To make up which sum there rests with his Majesty from the month of March, 1781, to the present month of March, inclusive, the sum of 13,000*l.*"

The following note is attached to the above and endorsed : '' Addition to the Private State ''

" There is due and yet to be paid by Lord Bute by agreement towards the expence of bringing his son, Colonel Stuart, into Parliament the sum of 1,000*l.* But besides the above disbursements actually paid as stated above, there are claims made for the expenses for the Surry election beyond the sum which has been already advanced and for the Liverpoole and the last election and petition for Colchester."

The following account is in the form of a booklet with a title page bearing the inscription : " Election Account from 1779 to April, 1782," and a preceding fly-leaf containing the following : " Memorandum : The following account[s] shew the payments made on account of the expences of elections progressively as the payments were made [and] what each place individually and separately cost."

His Majesty's Private Account.

Memorandum: The additional 1,000*l.* per month from the Civil List commenced in the month of November, 1777.

		l.	*s.*	*d*
1778				
January	Received from your Majesty for the months of November and December, 1777 . .	2,000		
6 February	Received from your Majesty for the months of January and February . . .	2,000		
26 June	Received from your Majesty for the months of March, April, May, and June . . .	4,000		
1779				
17 September	Received for 12 months from July, 1778, to June, 1779, inclusive . . .	12,000		
1780				
21 August	Received for 14 months from July, 1779, to August, 1780, inclusive . . .	14,000		
1781				
6 March	Received for 6 months from September, 1780, to February, 1781, inclusive	6,000		
	Total received from His Majesty	40,000		
	Received by Lord North otherwise as contributions towards the expences of the several elections	30,010	17	
1782				
April	Received from Lord Bute towards his son's election for Plympton .	1,000		
	Total received	71,010	17	
	Total disbursed . .	103,765	15	2
	Ballance due to Lord North .	32,754	18	2

		l.	*s.*	*d.*
1779				
18 September	Paid on account of Milborne Port .	3,374		
13 December	Paid on account of Hampshire contest .	2,000		
1780				
10 January	Paid on account of Stafford . . .	800		
12 May	Paid on account of Reading . .	300		
24 June	Paid on account of Milborne Port	3,197	10	
20 July	Paid on account of Bristol . . .	1,000		
28 July	Paid on account of Taunton . .	1,500		
26 August	Paid on account of Penryn . .	400		
29 August	Paid on account of Reading . . .	500		
1 September	Paid on account of Stafford . . .	700		
6 September	Paid on account of Harwich . .	100		
6 September	Paid on account of Reading	800		
6 September	Paid on account of Westminster	1,000		

1779		l.	s.	d.
6 September	Paid on account of Windsor	1,500		
9 September	Paid on account of Gloucester	500		
13 September	Paid on same account	1,000		
13 September	Paid on account of Westminster	1,500		
14 September	Paid on the like account	1,500		
21 September	Paid on the like account	2,000		
22 September	Paid on account of the City	1,500		
22 September	Paid on account of Selkirk, Orkney . .	300		
23 September	Paid on account of Surry	2,000		
17 October	Paid on account of Penryn	250		
26 October	Paid on account of Harwich	250		
29 November	Paid on account of Hythe	800		
5 December	Paid on account of St. Michaels	2,625		
8 December	Paid on account of Wootton Bassett . .	1,500		
8 December	Paid on account of Westminster 1,028 19 4			
	[Illegible, crossed through] [1] . 1,028 19 4	2,057	18	8
8 December	Paid on account of Aylesbury	1,500		
9 December	Paid on account of seats at Fowey, 2 at Plymouth, 2 at Lestwithiel, and 1 at Bossiney	18,000		
13 December	Paid on account of Horsham	5,325		
16 December	Paid on account of Gloucester	1,100		
16 December	Paid for several writs	50		
21 December	Paid on account of Surry	1,000		
22 December	Paid on account of Camelford	8,000		
1781				
24 January	Paid on account of Bristol	2,000		
26 January	Paid on account of Windsor	500		
26 January	Paid on account of Hythe	300		
10 February	Paid on account of Bristol	1,000		
10 February	Paid on account of Tamworth	1,000		
16 February	Paid on account of Orkney	315		
4 April	Paid on account of Tamworth	1,000		
4 April	Paid sundry expenses on account of Haslemere, Rochester, Portsmouth, Etc.	129	18	
7 April	Paid towards Gloucestershire	2,000		
14 April	Paid on account of Coventry	2,000		
10 May	Paid on account of Windsor	600		
12 May	Paid on account of Malmesbury	1,184	10	
19 May	Paid on account of Wootton Bassett . . .	500		
19 May	Paid on account of Bristol	1,000		
19 May	Paid on account of Taunton	1,000		
24 May	Paid on account of Plymouth	353	15	6
14 June	Paid for Midhurst	200		
23 June	Paid on account of Tamworth	2,000		
29 June	Paid on account of Bristol	1,000		
26 July	Paid for Orkney and for Edinburgh . . .	2,300		

---

[1] The bracketed item appears thus in pencil in the transcript.

	1781		*l.*	*s.*	*d.*
11 August	Paid on account of Milborne Port . . .	860		
22 August	Paid on account of Surry .	500		
23 August	Paid on account of City	1,000		
10 November	Paid on account of Surry	500		
13 November	Paid on account of petty expenses City . .	50		
4 December	Paid on account of Plymouth	930	12	
12 December	Paid for the City	800		
1782				
19 January	Paid for Lymington	3,000		
28 January	Paid on account of the City	858	17	6
31 January	Paid for Horsham reelection	309	15	6
22 February	Paid towards Barnstaple	1,500		
25 March	Paid for reelections, Plympton (J Stuart vice Salisbury) and Lestwithiel (Johnson vice Malden)	900		
	Paid ballance on settling Westminster .	65	7	
	Paid for reelection at Weymouth . . .	500		
	Paid ballance on account of Stafford . . .	41	11	
	Paid on account of Aylesbury . .	115		
		102,243	15	2
	Paid on account of Taunton	424		
	Paid for Newport, Isle of Wight . .	98		
		102,765	15	2
	Paid towards Sandwich	1,000		
		103,765	15	2

The following account is drawn up on a single sheet.

John Robinson Dr. to Lord North Cr. on Private Election Account.

	1778		*l.*	*s.*	*d.*
February 6	By cash received from Lord North, which he received from the King	2,000		
	1779				
September 18	By ditto	12,000		
	1780				
August 22	By ditto	14,000		
September 6	By ditto received for Lord Walsingham on this Act.	1,000		
September 6	By ditto from Mr. Pardoe	4,000		
September 6	By ditto from James Macpherson	4,000		
December 9	By ditto from Lord North, received by him from Mr Drummond	30,000		

1781		*l.*	*s.*	*d.*
March 6	By ditto from Lord North, received from his Majesty	6,000		
May 26	By ditto from Mr. Towson	3,500		
July 12	By ditto from Mr. Gybbon . .	800		
1782				
January 18	By ditto from Lord North from Messrs. Drummonds	16,710	17	
March 28	By ditto of Cornish revenues brought to this account to replace	8,658		
March 30	By ditto from Lord Bute	1,000		
	Received	103,668	17	
	By cash disbursed on account of various elections as by particulars thereof in account made up for his Majesty, vide which, amounting to	101,835	15	2
	Ballance due to Lord North . .	1,833	1	10

1784, August 19.—The King to John Robinson. " The very honorable part Mr. Robinson has acted in the late critical times, which by the assistance of Providence has wonderfully changed since the assembling of the New Parliament, deserves my expressing my thorough approbation of it previous to entering into the cause of this letter, therefore without farther preface, I shall shortly state the business I wish him to arrange for me and intrust him with the Original Papers which He is through Dalton to return to Me when He has done with them.

" Mr. Robinson is too well acquainted with the negligence of Lord North in the management of His private account with Me and of his great difficulty to close them which made it the 5th of May before I sent him a discharge by a letter of which the draft is enclosed though He resigned the 28th of March. By the most private Account He acknowledges my only being answerable for 13,000*l.* to Mr. Drummond. I accordingly in May paid 7,000*l.* to Mr. Drummond and desired the receipt might run in part of the 13,000*l.* Mr. Drummond wished to give me a simple receipt for 7,000*l.*, and Lord North sent Me his letter of the 16th of May by Lord Brudenell desiring I would be satisfied with it in that form as He would in a few months settle his own affairs and then explain the whole to Mr. Drummond. Thus it remained till last March when I wrote to Mr. Drummond on a further sum I wanted and stated this affair.   When I saw him to my great surprise He gave me the inclosed Paper and the Copy of the Note Lord North had signed by which I found Lord North has never yet explained the business ; I told Mr. Drummond all that had past with Lord North and said I would collect the Papers and get the business cleared up.

"What I therefore wish is that Mr. Robinson will shew Mr. Drummond that Lord North Acknowledged my having nothing further to pay than the 13,000l. of which 7,000l. is already returned and let Mr. Drummond shew to Lord North His original letter of May 16th, 1782. It is not necessary for Mr. Drummond to mention the channel through which I have sent him this voucher, consequently Mr. Robinson will not appear ; my reason for chusing him is that though I have both public and private reasons to be displeased with Lord North I do not wish so shameful a conduct should be known farther than to prevent Mr. Drummond being a loser."

1784, October 24.—Henry Drummond to John Robinson. Endorsed : "Most Private. R[eceived] 5 p.m. by Mr. Drummond's servant and answered immediately. J. R." "Sunday afternoon 3 o'clock   I have just received the enclosed note to me which is strong indeed against our old friend. I think I had better send *no* answer to his M[ajesty], and you will say when I shall wait upon you. If Tuesday will do I shall be at Charing Cross at one o'clock and remain always, my Dear Sir, Your much obliged friend etc. Pray let me know by the bearer whether I should send an answer to his M[ajesty] and what answer would you advise."

1784, October 24.—Windsor. The King to John Robinson. " I put thorough confidence in Mr Robinson's seeing that the Bond is every way proper, as also the state of interest on the sums that have been borrowed. I enclose the 6,000l which I desire Mr. Robinson will pay to Mr. Drummond and get the proper receipt ; I shall take the same method of making the subsequent payments ; when the bond is ready I trust it will be sent for my signing "

1784, October 26.—Syon Hill. John Robinson to the King. " Mr. Robinson in obedience to your Majesty's commands has prepared on stampt paper for your Majesty's signature the bond and the declaration transmitted through Mr. Drummond. Mr. Robinson has examined the account of interest with Mr. Drummond, and Mr. R[obinson] hopes both the account and the bond, and the declaration, which is similar to that Mr. Drummond informs Mr.

R[obinson] your Majesty was pleased to give on taking the ten thousand pounds, are correct and right.   Mr Robinson has the honour to transmit the papers herewith, and also a receipt from Mr Drummond for the 6,000*l* committed to Mr. Robinson's charge to pay Mr. Drummond.   When your Majesty shall have been pleased to sign the papers and to return them Mr. Robinson will immediately exchange the securities with Mr. Drummond and transmit the old ones to your Majesty.   Your Majesty will be pleased to affix your seal to the bond after your signature, and to have one witness at least to the attestation.   And likewise to insert in the blank left in the declaration the sum in the Bank consolidated annuities in trust for your Majesty."

[UNDATED MEMORANDUM IN THE KING'S HAND.]

October, 1784 .	6,000*l*.
March, 1785	5,000*l*.
October, (1785)	6,000*l*.
March, 1786	5,000*l*.
March, 1777 [1787 ?] .	5,000*l*.[1]
	33,000

" Received 33,000*l*. and in a Subsequent Payment will discharge the Interest of this sum.

" If Mr. Drummond chuses to be paid in more frequent installments provided the Sum in each Year is not beyond what is here for each Year proposed, it will not be objected."

[1] An item of 6,000*l*. for October, 1786, was obviously omitted.

THE PARLIAMENTARY ELECTION
OF 1784

SECTION III

THE PARLIAMENTARY ELECTION OF 1784

THE following " State " is perhaps the most detailed description
extant of the actual forces represented in the parliaments
of the latter part of the eighteenth century. Nowhere else has
the real character of a parliamentary election been revealed so
clearly. These memoranda were made subsequent to the passage
of Fox's India Bill by the House of Commons and previous to
the dismissal of Fox and North after its rejection by the House
of Lords It seems likely that the work was done by Robinson
in the second week in December, 1783.

The decisive question with Pitt in declining the offer of the king
in the spring of 1783 seems to have been the improbability that
he could command the support of a majority in the House of Commons at that time. The persons who were active in persuading
him to undertake in December that which he had declined in March
appear to have used the evidence here provided by Robinson as
a part of their argument.

The first " pro," " hopeful," " doubtful," and " con " columns
on the left indicate Robinson's estimate of the probable attitude
of the members of the House as it existed in the fall of 1783 in
case the king should dismiss the Coalition ministry and Pitt should
take office ; the second columns indicate the probable attitude
of the members of a new parliament, elected after a dissolution
preceded by the dismissal of the Coalition and the accession of
Pitt.

The task of Robinson in making these estimates was the more
difficult in that there had been a radical realignment of political
groups since the general election of 1780. Many members who

acted with Fox and North as friends of the latter had come in for government constituencies or aided by government influence and would naturally lose their seats with North out of office. Moreover, the Chathamite group, now led by Pitt and acting with the friends of the king, were in.1780 associated with the Rockingham Whigs. Finally, the elimination of the revenue officers from the list of voters by the measure passed in the administration of Rockingham made Robinson himself uncertain as to the state of influence in some constituencies, like the Cinque Ports, of which he had formerly been sure.

The italicized comments in the left-hand marginal column under the list of English counties appear in the transcript in pencil and were apparently so in the original.

ENGLISH COUNTIES.

~ 178?	Pro.	Hopeful.	Doubtful.	Con.	Pro.	Hopeful.	Doubtful.	Con.	
Bedfordshire. .				2				2	The same members reelected and both *con.*
Berkshire . . *Neither hopeful*		1		1		1		1	Probably the same members and that they will stand as classed.
Buckinghamshire *Future* 1 *D*				2				2	This is canvassed as if the same members. But others can best judge of this.
Cambridgeshire . *Both pro*	1		1		1		1		Most likely the same members again and as classed.
Cheshire . . *Cotton pro* *Crewe con*		1		1		1		1	The same members. Crew *con* but Sir Robert Cotton might perhaps without reckoning too much be classed *pro* ; as safer however only classed hopeful.
Cornwall . . *Both pro*	1	1			1	1			Same members again.
Cumberland . . 1 *D future*	1			1	1			1	Whether the same members may be again returned here is uncertain, or whether there may be a contest. But if there should [be] one, it may be doubtful whether Sir H[enry] Fletcher would come in against some gentleman of the country if

ENGLISH COUNTIES—*continued.*

	Pro.	Hopeful.	Doubtful.	Con.	Pro.	Hopeful.	Doubtful.	Con.	
									they should stand. However, as all is uncertain, it is classed *con* in a future parliament also.
Derbyshire . . *one pro* } *both* *one con* }			1	1	1			1	The old members probably. Mr. Curzon at present may vote *con*, but on a change would, it is apprehended, be for. Lord Scarsdale's situation and Lord Gower.
Devonshire . . Both	1	1			1	1			The same members, and it is thought are properly classed.
Dorsetshire . . 1 *H*, 1 *D*	1	1			1	1			The same again and as the last unless Mr. Sturt has expectations for his son who is gone to India.
Durham . . . *pro* 1 *cannot attend* 1 *con* 1 *pro* } *future* 1 *h* }		1		1	1			1	The same members probably unless Sir Thomas Clavering should decline. If he did so, a friend in the same interest may succeed and be also hopeful. Sir J[ohn] Eden will be against.
Yorkshire . 1 *pro*, 1 *H* both	1			1	1		1		Mr. Duncombe will most likely be reelected. It is said Sir George Saville wished to get his nephew Foljambe elected, but that this is not acceptable. How it may turn out is uncertain, and therefore it is classed as doubtful.
Essex. . . . 1 *pro*, 1 *con*		1		1	1			1	The same members will most likely be returned again, and it is apprehended that they are classed as they will stand.
Gloucestershire .			1	1			1	1	Most likely the same gentlemen. Mr. Dutton has generally supported Lord North.
Herefordshire . 1 *pro*, 1 *con*	1		1		1		1		Probably the same gentlemen again.
Hertfordshire .			1	1			1	1	Probably the same again. Halsey is put down doubtful, but if Lord Salisbury is with, may be very hopeful.

ENGLISH COUNTIES—*continued*.

	Pro.	Hopeful.	Doubtful.	Con.	Pro.	Hopeful	Doubtful	Con.	
Huntingdonshire 2 *con both times*	1			1	1			1	The same members again Probably Lord Hinchingbroke might be got *pro* with arrangement.
Kent	2				2				The same members again and may both be *pro*, were so in the East India Bill.
Lancashire . . 1 *pro*, 1 *con*		1		1	1			1	The same members again. Sir Thomas Egerton would on a change, it is thought, be *pro*.
Leicestershire . 1 *pro, Hungerford H*		2				2			These two gentlemen are thought both to be hopeful and probably will be reelected.
Lincolnshire . .				2				2	The same again probably and perhaps both against.
Middlesex . 1 *pro*, 1 *con*			1	1			1	1	*Perhaps* the same gentlemen Mr Byng certainly *against* Mr. Wilkes's support of any government is very uncertain, because the safety of his situation depends on his watching as he calls it all administrations and having no apparent connection with any, but taking the side of all popular questions. Therefore he is classed as doubtful.
Monmouthshire .			1	1		1		1	Mr. John Morgan will certainly come in again and as to him vide the remark on this family's connections in Breconshire in Wales Mr. Hanbury is in a very ill state of health, and for that and other causes he is gone abroad. His life has been thought precarious for sometime, and it has been suggested that in case of his death Mr. Nevill, whose family property is large in that county, might be acceptable to the country, and Mr. Nevill's standing on such event has been in contemplation.

ENGLISH COUNTIES—*continued*

	Pro.	Hopeful.	Doubtful	Con.	Pro.	Hopeful.	Doubtful	Con	
									Whether Mr. Hanbury will decline in case of a vacancy cannot be ascertained until he can be wrote to, nor whether the county would in the situation of Mr. Hanbury call on Mr. Nevill, but it is expected Mr. Nevill will stand, by some of his friends, in either case.
Norfolk . . . 1 *pro*, 1 *con*		1		1		1		1	Probably the same members will be again returned. Mr. Coke's connections etc. carry him dead—*con*—Sir Edward Astley will often [be] *for* and perhaps sometimes against
Northampshire .	1	1				1	1		Most likely the same gentlemen and that they may be classed as marked. Mr Knightley's wish is to support government.
Northumberland		1	1			1	1		The same gentlemen will be returned most likely. Lord Algernoon(*sic*) seldom attends and is therefore only put *hopeful*. Sir William Middleton does not attend much, but his part is more doubtful.
Nottinghamshire 1 *con*, 1 *D*			2					2	Most likely the same members and most likely both *con*
Oxfordshire . . 1 *pro*, 1 *con*			1	1	1			1	Most likely the same members. Lord Charles Spencer is now *con* as in office, but on a change would be *for*. Lord Wenman it is thought would also be favourable but as uncertain is classed doubtful
Rutlandshire . 1 *pro*, 1 *cannot attend*	1		1		1		1		Probably the same members Mr. Brudenel was against the East India Bill. Mr. Noel's ideas are not known, but he does not attend much.
Shropshire . . 2 *pro*		2				2			The two Mr. Hills would probably be returned again, and it is thought that they may be classed as hopeful.

ENGLISH COUNTIES—*continued.*

	Pro.	Hopeful.	Doubtful.	Con.	Pro.	Hopeful.	Doubtful.	Con.	
Somersetshire . 1 *pro*, 1 *cannot attend* 1 *pro*, 1 *H*		1		1	1			1	If the same two members should be again returned it is thought they will stand the same as now, but on the idea of Mr. Cox's death, it was said that Lord Hinton would offer himself. If so he probably will be *pro.*
Southampton County	1			1	1			1	The same gentlemen again most likely and stand as classed.
Staffordshire .	1			1	1			1	Probably the same members and stand as classed.
Suffolk . . . 1 *pro*, 1 *con*		1		1	1			1	The same gentlemen again most likely and act as classed.
Surrey . . .	1			1	1			1	Probably the same gentlemen, and they will continue to act as they do now.
Sussex . . .	1			1	1			1	Probably the same persons will be again returned, though an opposition in Sussex is not impossible. Lord Surrey wished much on the last vacancy to raise one if I had given the least way in it, and Lord Abergavenny was not pleased I did not. Sir Godfrey Webster may probably bustle.
Warwickshire . 1 *Sh, pro,* 1 *D*			1	1			1	1	Probably the same gentlemen again. Sir G[eorge Augustus William] Shuckburgh is much connected with Mr. Fox. Sir Robert Lawley's sentiments are not well known, therefore classed doubtful.
Westmoreland	2				2				The same gentlemen most likely, and both *pro.*
Worcestershire .			1	1			1	1	The old members. Mr. Foley certainly against, Mr. Lygon not unlikely to be generally *for,* but however classed doubtful.
Wiltshire. . .		2				2			Very likely to be again returned. They are moderate gentlemen, wish to preserve the constitution, and it is thought may with civility be friendly.
[Total English Counties]	18	19	12	31	22	18	11	29	

ENGLISH BOROUGHS, OPEN.

	Pro.	Hopeful	Doubtful	Con.	Pro.	Hopeful	Doubtful	Con.	
Bedford . . .	1		1		1		1		Open. Sir Robert Bernard might get in.
Reading . . .	1			1	1			1	But same members most likely to be returned unless Major Walter should choose to stand.
Abingdon . .		1					1		But most likely the member would be returned in the same interest.
Windsor . . .	1		1		1			1	But same members probably.
Wallingford . .	2				1			1	Most likely a contest and perhaps Cator succeed.
Aylesbury . .	1	1			1	1			But unless Lord Temple should oppose will probably reelect same members. But, query, whether Mr. Bacon would desire to come in again, though personally lik[ed] there.
Marlow . . .	1		1		1			1	Mr. Clayton probably would be elected again, but it is very doubtful who would be the other.
Cambridge .	1		1		1			1	Doubtful who might be elected there. Neither of the present members very secure.
Chester .	2				2				Most likely to be the present members again.
Truro. . .	1			1				2	Probably will be fought between Lord Falmouth and Sir Francis Bassett.
Bodmyn . . .	1		1		1			1	Most probable (sic) the same members.
Helston . . .	2				2				Very doubtful how this would be, for the charter is not yet accepted and some of the old corporators yet left Lord Carmarthen's if the charter was settled.
Penryn . . .				2				2	Sir Francis Bassett supposes himself secure, but yet there is an interest here who will most probably oppose him.

ENGLISH BOROUGHS, OPEN—*continued*.

	Pro.	Hopeful.	Doubtful.	Con.	Pro.	Hopeful.	Doubtful.	Con.	
Callington . .				2			1	1	Lord Orford claims to have the borough, but it is not admitted, for there is another gentleman, Mr. Coryton, near the place who disputes it, and probably there will be a contest, which was prevented last time, both gentlemen being friends to government.
Carlisle . .	1			1	1			1	But probably will reelect the same members.
Derby . .				2				2	Most likely the same members.
Tiverton . .	1			1	1				Probably will reelect the same members.
Honiton . .	1			1	1	1			Very doubtful who may be elected with Sir George Yonge, nor is he quite safe.
Plymouth . .			1	1	2				Most likely will reelect Sir Frederick Rogers ; the other member through the admiralty.
Totnes . . .			1	1			2		Duke of Bolton 1, certain ; the other rather open, but Judge Buller seems to have a great weight there.
Barnstaple . .	2				1	1			Very likely will have a contest, Cleveland Bassett and Devaynes.
Exeter . . .	1			1	1			1	Very likely the same members.
Dorchester . .			1	1	1			1	Most likely the old members.
Bridport . . .	1			1	1			1	Very uncertain who will be returned.
Shaftesbury . .	1		1		1	1			Very likely to be carried by the old members.
Poole	2				2				Probably the old members, but not certainly so ; there may be a contest. Query, Mr. Pitt gone abroad, Gulstone ill.
Durham . .	1			1	1			1	Most likely the same members.
Beverley .				2				2	Very likely the old members unless Sir Charles Thompson should think it right to stand.

ENGLISH BOROUGHS, OPEN—*continued*.

	Pro.	Hopeful.	Doubtful.	Con.	Pro.	Hopeful.	Doubtful.	Con.	
Heddon . . .	1			1	2				Mr. Chaytor is well liked there and very likely will be elected again. Government may get the other with attention, particularly if another person vice Atkinson does not get fisc (*sic*) in it.
Pomfret . .	1			1		2			It is hard to say what will become of it, but it will be fought again.
Scarborough .	1			1	2				Probably the same members, but government has, or ought to have a great weight there Mr. Phipps came in on their interest.
York	1			1	1			1	Probably the same members.
Hull . .	1			1	1	1			Mr. Wilberforce most probably, and government can carry the other with attention and exertion.
Colchester . .	1			1	1		1		Perhaps the same members, but very uncertain.
Malden .	2				2				Probably the same members.
Harwich . .	1			1	2				By the disfranchisement of the revenue officers rendered hazardous, but probably Mr. R[obinson] and another friend of government may be, elected.
Tewkesbury .	1		1		1		1		Probably the same members.
Gloucester .				2				2	Perhaps the same members, but may have a contest.
Hereford . .	1			1	1			1	Probably the same members.
Leominster . .	2				2				Probably the same members.
Hertford . .	1			1	1		1		Very like to have a contest between Mr. Calvert and Baker.
St. Albans .				2				2	Probably the same members.
Rochester .		1		1		1		1	Probably the same members
Maidstone .	1		1		1	1			Probably the same members
Canterbury .	2				2				Probably the same members
Lancaster		1		1			1	1	Very likely the same
Preston . . .		1		1			1	1	Very likely to have a contest but classed as if the old members were to come in.

ENGLISH BOROUGHS, OPEN—*continued*.

	Pro.	Hopeful.	Doubtful.	Con.	Pro.	Hopeful.	Doubtful.	Con.	
Liverpoole	1	1			1	1			Probably the same members.
Wigan				2				2	Perhaps the same gentlemen.
Leicester			1	1			1	1	Probably the same members.
Grantham	1	1			1	1			Most likely the same members.
Boston		1		1		1		1	Most likely the same members.
Grimsby				2				2	Will very likely be carried by Mr. Pelham, both members, though there may be a contest.
Lincoln		1		1	1	1			Probably the same members, but there may be a contest against Cawthorne.
Westminster			1	1			1	1	Very open : two good men would run hard if not turn out both the present members.
London	2	1	1		2		1	1	Probably the same members unless an attack can be made on Sawbridge from present circumstances.
Monmouth	1				1				Abroad. Would be returned again until a son of the Duke of Beaufort comes of age.
Lynn	1				1			1	Probably the same unless Mr. Thomas Walpole's son should come in in the room of his father.
Yarmouth				2				2	Probably the same members.
Norwich			1	1	1			1	Mr. Bacon is so ill he can't attend and can't live long ; perhaps may not wish to come in again. Gentlemen have been canvassing to succeed him again, but, query, Mr. Thurlow stand.
Peterborough	1			1	1			1	Lord Fitzwilliams has weight here ; may be a contest, but thought likely that the same members will come in.
Northampton	1			1	1			1	Lord Compton will most probably come in in the room of Mr. Rodney. But the Northampton and Spencer interests will join, although Sir George Robinson may make a contest and press them.

ENGLISH BOROUGHS, OPEN—*continued.*

	Pro	Hopeful	Doubtful	Con.	Pro.	Hopeful	Doubtful	Con.	
Newcastle-upon-Tyne		1	1			1	1		Probably the same members.
Berwick . . .				2		2			Probably the same members.
East Retford .		1	1		1	1			Most likely the same members.
Newark . .	1	1				2			The same members.
Nottingham . .	1	1				2			The same members.
Oxford University		2				2			The same.
Oxford City . .	1			1	1			1	The same.
Shrewsbury . .		2				2			Probably the old members.
Ludlow .	1			1	1			1	Most likely the same members.
Bridgenorth .				2			1	1	The old members
Wenlock . . .				2				2	The old members.
Bishop's Castle .	2				1			1	The old members
Taunton . .			2					2	This borough is very open, and there may be a contest, but if the old members succeed they may be reckoned *hopeful.*
Ivelchester . .	1		1		2				This borough is open, but notwithstanding the weight of interest is with the old members, who will be *with,* it is expected.
Milborne Port .	1	1			1	1			Will probably be the old members or gentlemen elected by the same interest.
Wells . . .		2				2			Probably the same members.
Bridgewater . .		2				2			Probably the same members.
Bath	1	1			1	1			The old members again probably and that they would stand as classed.
Bristol . . .		2				2			The present members for this place would stand the best chance of being again elected, though an opposition may arise, promoted by Mr. Burke's friends, and being aided by government these two gentlemen if elected would certainly at least be *hopeful* if not entirely for administration.
Cirencester .	1	1			1	1			This borough is not a close one, but it is much under the influ-

ENGLISH BOROUGHS, OPEN—*continued*.

	Pro.	Hopeful.	Doubtful.	Con.	Pro.	Hopeful.	Doubtful	Con.	
							-		once of Lord Bathurst and Mr. Blackwell ; therefore the present members will be reckoned ; Lord Apsley certainly *pro*, and Mr. Blackwell very much so, and almost always therefore may at least be classed hopeful.
Andover . . .		1		1	1			1	Is not a close borough, but the present members are almost sure of being reelected and may be classed as marked.
Stockbridge . .				2				2	This borough requires attention and management, which may make an alteration very material in it both in the present and future parliament, but in the present state of things it is in both cases classed *against*.
Southampton	2				2				An open borough, but the present members, supported by the government, have the interest. They have thought themselves neglected by Lord North and ill used by Portland. They stay away, at least Sloane does always. But it is thought in both events with civility they are hopeful.
Stafford . .				2				2	This is very open. An opportunity easily made to affect one certainly, perhaps both, though classed as *con*.
Litchfield . .	1			1	1			1	The present members most likely will be again returned. Lord Gower's man *with*, Mr. Anson *against*.
Ipswich . . .			2					2	The old members will probably be returned here. The one, Mr. Wollaston is abroad. Mr. Staunton is an uncertain man, so classed doubtful.

ENGLISH BOROUGHS, OPEN—*continued.*

	Pro.	Hopeful.	Doubtful.	Con.	Pro.	Hopeful.	Doubtful.	Con.	
Aldborough, Suffolk		1		1	2				The same members, or one and a friend, it is thought with attention, if a particularly agreeable person, not otherwise, and therefore they are classed as they stand at present, but hereafter as both hopeful.
Sudbury . . .			1	1				2	As open as the day and night too, and it is hard to say who may come, whether Marriot and Blake or Crespigny and some other person, therefore it is left doubtful
Bury				2			1	1	For one member this depends on the Duke of Grafton, and it is apprehended may be *hopeful.* Sir Charles Davers will come in for the other and be against, it is apprehended.
Guildford . .	1			1	2				Most probable will return its old members who now stand divided but on a change will, it is thought, be both *pro.*
Southwark . .	2				2				Very likely to be its old members and that they will both be *for.*
Shoreham .		2					2		This place is now very open, but yet government with management have considerable weight there notwithstanding it being so laid open. The two gentlemen who now represent this place are well inclined and rather attached to government ; with civility they may be made steady and with fairness may be classed very hopeful in either event.
Arundel . . .			1	1				2	Lord Surry and his family have the natural interest here, and his Lordship has been paying attention to this place of late,

ENGLISH BOROUGHS, OPEN—*continued.*

	Pro.	Hopeful.	Doubtful.	Con.	Pro.	Hopeful.	Doubtful.	Con.	
									but the election rests in the inhabitant householders. His Lordship's weight may carry one, but that even will require *attention,* and with *great attention* and management one seat may probably be in future obtained, if not both.
Lewes . . .			1	1	1			1	This is open, probably though the same members may be again returned, but if so *one* or *both* perhaps may be made steady with management, though not ventured to class them as yet so favourably.
Chichester	1		1	1				1	Whether the present members will be again elected here is very difficult to say. The last contest was severe and near run although fought under disadvantages. It is most probable there will be an opposition again, and therefore it is not ventured to class these otherwise than as they now stand.
Warwick .	1		1		2				It is not likely that Lord Warwick will as yet recover the borough from Mr. Ladbroke, and therefore probably the same members may be again returned, and therefore they are classed thus in future, and Mr. Greville, not being very sanguine, is at present put doubtful.
Coventry . .				2			1	1	Is very open, but probably the two parties for quietness will reelect their present members : at present both against, but on any change one may be classed doubtful.

ENGLISH BOROUGHS, OPEN—*continued*.

	Pro.	Hopeful.	Doubtful.	Con.	Pro.	Hopeful	Doubtful	Con	
Evesham . .		1	1			1	1		Probably the same members, and as they have not appeared to take any decided line they are so classed.
Worcester .	1	1			1	1			Probably the same gentlemen will be again returned. Mr. Rous seems with ; Mr. Ward with civility may be steadied.
New Sarum . .	1		1		1		1		Probably the old members who, it is apprehended, may be so classed.
Devizes . . .		2				2			It is probable the same members will be elected again and that they may very fairly be classed hopeful, for their inclinations are with government
Chippenham .		1		1		1		1	It is very likely that the present members will be again returned. Mr. Dawkins is and has generally been connected with the present administration. Mr. Fludyer is scarce yet settled, but from connections, although brother to Sir Samuel, may be classed *hopeful*.
Cricklade . .			1	1			1	1	It is very hard indeed to class this borough or to say who is likely to be returned for it, it is now laid so open. The Bolingbroke family have interest in that part of the country, and through that Mr. St. John was elected. Whether he can also carry a colleague is uncertain, and therefore in future, as in present, the members are classed *doubtful* and *con*. Benfield is abroad.
Hindon . . .	1		1		1		1		Mr. Kenyon, it is probable, may come in here again on the Beckford interest, and he or young Mr. Beckford or both

ENGLISH BOROUGHS, OPEN—*continued.*

	Pro.	Hopeful.	Doubtful.	Con.	Pro.	Hopeful.	Doubtful.	Con.	
									may come in again, but it [is] very *open* indeed, and from that it is uncertain, it is not therefore ventured to class it more than one *for,* one *doubtful.* Mr. Wraxhall will have little chance there again.
Wootton Bassett				2		1	1		Lord Bolingbroke's family have weight here by attention and management General St. John may again come in for *one* The other is hopeful to be got by attention.
CINQUE PORTS Dover . .				2				2	Although it is the wish of the inhabitants of Dover because it is so much their interest, and although if a good man could be found to stand there he would probably carry it, yet as Lord North is Lord Warden there may be doubts about it, and therefore both members are classed as they stand now, *against*
Hastings . . .		1		1	2				The disfranchising bill has made great alterations in this and other boroughs, yet it is hoped that this borough with great attention may as formerly be got to return two friends, but this can't be known until the time comes for conversation
Rye . .				2	2				Same observations as to Hastings precisely
Seaford . .				2			2		Same observations as to Hastings, only this borough, it is apprehended, stands more precarious
Sandwich . .				2	1	1			This is a borough of contests. Government has a pretty strong interest there and suc-

ENGLISH BOROUGHS, OPEN—*continued.*

	Pro.	Hopeful.	Doubtful.	Con.	Pro.	Hopeful.	Doubtful.	Con.	
									ceeded, at the last fight, the opposite party, but there may be another contest. Mr. Stephens is probably safe, but Sir Richard Sutton not so sure, particularly if he should not be supported by government. Mr. Brett stood there last.
Hythe . . .				2	2				With the support of government the present members will make their election good here again ; and they deserve it, for they are very steady and always well inclined to support government and may as such be classed *pro.*
New Romney .	1		1		1	1			This borough is Sir Edward Deering's. He will most likely return himself and Mr. Jackson again, and as things change, Sir Edward is not obstinate.
Winchelsea . .		1		1	2				The Speaker and Mr. Nesbit. This borough is now, it is feared, in a bad state indeed, and scarce any good voters in it. It was on a compromise between government and Nesbit, and the Speaker was brought in at a very trifling expence and some annual payments. The revenue officers having been struck off leaves scarce a good voter, and besides that, this borough has been so much neglected for near two years past that it is scarce known in what situation it stands until it is again examined. However, as Nesbit is somewhat hampered and wishes to be with administration, it is thought with attention it may be got right again

G

ENGLISH BOROUGHS, OPEN—*continued.*

	Pro.	Hopeful	Doubtful	Con.	Pro.	Hopeful	Doubtful	Con.	
Cambridge University				2				2	and made *pro*, though probably with some bustle and expence. If the same members, Mr. Townshend and Mr. Mansfield, should be again elected, will in future also be *con.* But if on a change Lord Euston and Mr. Pitt should stand for this University, it is more than probable that, circumstances having so changed, one or both of these gentlemen will succeed. However, from this being in a state of uncertainty, this place is marked as now, *con.*
[Total Open Boroughs]	70	40	30	92	84	54	36	58	

ENGLISH BOROUGHS, CLOSE

	Pro.	Hopeful	Doubtful	Con.	Pro.	Hopeful	Doubtful	Con.	
Buckingham . .	2				2				Lord Temple's.
Wycombe . .	1	1			1	1			Lord Shelburne and Mr. Waller.
Wendover . .				2			2		Because with attention this borough *may be got.*
Agmondesham .		2						2	This is the Drake's family borough, and they will be re-elected.
Launceston . .	1		1		2				The Duke of Northumberland and Sir John Jervais came in on an arrangement. Whether these two gentlemen may come in again is uncertain, but it is thought the Duke will bring in friends
Liskeard . . .	1				1		2		This borough is under the influence of Mr. Elliot who would most likely bring in Mr. Salt again and who would be with administration. He may not.

ENGLISH BOROUGHS, CLOSE—*continued*

	Pro.	Hopeful.	Doubtful.	Con.	Pro.	Hopeful.	Doubtful.	Con.	
									probably bring in Mr. Tollemache again, but a friend to administration, as Mr. Tollemache's connections are with those, (the Spencers), who may not be so steady. This borough is therefore canvassed in a future parliament as 2 *pro.*
Lostwithiel	1			1	2				In Lord Edgecumbe's arrangement. His Lordship's consequence is very considerable. He or his agent or both must be talked to. Notice must be taken of him. Attention must be paid to his interest, and all his weight will be secured for steady friends; therefore classed in future as *pros.*
Saltash .	1			1	2				Under the arrangement of government with attention at the moment
East Looe	1	1			2				Mr. Buller's, senior, who most likely will come in himself and may by civility be made steady. Mr. Hamilton, Lord Abercorn's heir, who is just returned, strongly *for.*
West Looe	1	1			2				Mr. Buller, junior, probably Mr. Cocks. If Sir William James, he should be made steady.
Grampound .			2		2				Mr. Elliot's influence. The present members were chose on the recommendation of Lord Rockingham, it is apprehended, and therefore act with the present administration. Mr. Elliot will probably elect two steady friends.
Camelford . .	1	1			2				Is under the influence of Mr. Phillips. He has some engagements to one of the present members, it is apprehended,

ENGLISH BOROUGHS, CLOSE—*continued.*

	Pro	Hopeful	Doubtful	Con.	Pro.	Hopeful	Doubtful	Con.	
									but whether to the other is uncertain. But if they come in they may be made *for,* it is thought. If not, with great attention, he will, it is apprehended, bring in two friends.
Tregony .	1	1			2				Lord Falmouth with civility may, it is hoped, be prevailed on to bring in two friends, but whether the same two members is uncertain.
Bossiney . . .		1	1		1	1			Is between Lady Bute and Lord Edgecumbe. Lady Bute will probably name one of her own family. Lord Edgecumbe, as observed before, may recommend a friend.
St. Ives . .	1	1			2				Under the arrangement of Mr. Praed. The present member, Mr. Praed, will come in himself, but if Mr. Smith should not come in, Mr. Praed will, it is thought, choose a steady friend and probably be so himself.
Fowey . . .			1	1	1		1		Between Mr. Rashleigh and Lord Edgecumbe. Mr. Rashleigh will come in again himself. Lord Edgecumbe, as above observed, will bring in a friend it is hoped.
St. Germains .	1			1	2				Under Mr. Elliot's arrangement. Will, it is apprehended, bring in a steady friend with himself.
Mitchell . .				2	1			1	Lord Falmouth and Sir Francis Bassett. Sir Francis will bring his friend in the room of Mr. Hall and probably be *against.* Lord Falmouth may probably be prevailed on to bring in a friend vice Hanger.
Newport . .			1	1	2				The Duke of Northumberland's. How far the Duke may find

ENGLISH BOROUGHS, CLOSE—*continued.*

	Pro.	Hopeful.	Doubtful.	Con.	Pro.	Hopeful.	Doubtful.	Con.	
									himself bound to reelect the present members, having sat so shortly, it cannot be guessed at, but if not entanglement of that sort, it is hoped he may be prevailed upon to return two steady friends.
St. Mawes .	1	1			2				This borough belongs to the two present members who probably will represent it again, and Mr. Boscawen may be made steady.
Cockermouth .	2				2				Sir James Lowther. Same members perhaps, or two other friends.
Ashburton .		2			2				Lord Orford and Sir Robert Palke's borough. Most probably will be the same members and will be friends.
Dartmouth . .			1	1	1		1		Is under the care of Mr. Holdsworth; will come in himself and probably Mr. Brett or some other friend of government.
Okehampton .		1		1	1			1	Is the Duke of Bedford's and Lord Spencer's; they probably will return the same members.
Beeralston . .				2	2				The Duke of Northumberland's. The present members are both *against*, but unless as before observed some engagements made, the Duke, it is hoped, may bring in two friends.
Plympton . .				2	2				Lord Edgecumbe's arrangement; may, it is hoped, be prevailed to return *two* friends.
Tavistock . .				2				2	The Duke of Bedford's, who probably will return the old members.
Lyme. . . .		2			2				Lord Westmoreland's family; if any change may be hopeful In future very likely to be more than hopeful with civility and management.

ENGLISH BOROUGHS, CLOSE—*continued*.

	Pro.	Hopeful.	Doubtful.	Con.	Pro.	Hopeful.	Doubtful.	Con.	
Weymouth Etc.			2	2	4				Mr. Stuart has the arrangement of these boroughs. He is pay-master of the marines and his brother receiver general of Dorsetshire. The family used always to receive the recommendation of two from government and one of the family come in and support. They then had only three seats. With great attention it is hoped Mr. Stuart would act a similar part and bring in 3 friends and himself.
Wareham .	1			1	2				This borough of Mr. Calcraft's is under the care of Mr. Lucas, the commissioner of excise, and it is apprehended that he may be prevailed on to bring in two friends.
Corf Castle . .	1	1			2				Mr. Banke's and Mr. Bond's borough, who will come in themselves and may be classed *for*. Mr. Bankes is most certainly ; Mr. Bond is always well inclined.
Aldborough, Yorkshire			1	1	2				This borough belongs to the Duke of Newcastle. Mellish has Nottinghamshire connection with Portland Etc. and is doubtful. Sir S[amuel] Fludyer is always against. The Duke therefore, it is hoped, will either bring in two steady friends or steady Mr. Mellish. Sir Samuel will scarce be brought in again.
Boroughbridge .		2				2			The Duke of Newcastle's borough ; hoped as above for his bringing in two friends.
Knaresborough .				2				2	The Duke of Devonshire. Same members or others of same sentiments.

ENGLISH BOROUGHS, CLOSE—*continued.*

	Pro.	Hopeful.	Doubtful.	Con.	Pro.	Hopeful.	Doubtful.	Con.	
Malton . .				2				2	Lord Fitzwilliam's. Same.
Northallerton .		1		1	2				Mr. Lascelles's and Mr. Pears's borough. Same members. Mr. Lascelles, it is thought, is hopeful now but in case of a change would steadily support.
Richmond .	1			1				2	Sir Thomas Dundas's borough.
Ripon .	1	1			1	1			Late Mr Aislabie's. Same members most likely will be returned and may be so classed.
Thirsk . .				2			2		Sir Thomas Frankland's borough ; was secured by attention last time ; may be so this perhaps, but will require good management.
Weobly . .		2				2			Lord Weymouth ; the same or as good friends, it is apprehended
Huntingdon . .				2				2	Lord Sandwich's, who will return the old members or those who will go with him.
Queenborough				2	2				Under the arrangement of government to bring in two members.
Clithero . . .				2				2	Mr. Lister's borough ; is supposed entirely closed now. Same members most likely.
Newton, Lancashire				2				2	Mr Leigh's borough ; same members returned most likely, and at present so classed.
Stamford. . .	1	1			2				Lord Exeter's influence and most likely will return the same members.
Thetford . .				2				2	The Duke of Grafton.
Castlerising . .			1	1			1	1	Lord Orford and Miss Howard, married to Mr. Bagot, now Mr. Howard. Is receiver general for London and Middlesex and might be talked to.
Brackley . .			1	1	2				The Duke of Bridgewater.
Higham Ferrars .				1				1	Lord Fitzwilliam's.
Morpeth . . .				2			2		Lord Carlisle.

ENGLISH BOROUGHS, CLOSE—*continued.*

	Pro	Hopeful	Doubtful	Con	Pro.	Hopeful	Doubtful	Con.	
Woodstock . .				2			1	1	Probably the Duke of Marlborough will again return the same members, and although Lord Parker's inclinations as Lord Macclesfield certainly are with government, yet Lord Parker being in the Prince's household can only be classed as doubtful.
Banbury				1				1	Either the same member or one of the family.
Minehead	1	1			1	1			This borough belongs to the family of Lutterell of Minehead. Probably one seat that may be got, and Mr. Beaufoy might be again returned. However, until that is certain only classed hopeful and doubtful.
Winchester .	1	1			1	1			This borough is under the influence of the Duke of Chandos and Mr. Penton between whom there is an agreement. The Duke will therefore recommend one, supposed a steady friend. Mr. Penton feels himself neglected and hurt and therefore may be classed hopeful, but he had formerly a wish to quit parliament. The seat, therefore, might perhaps be got.
Portsmouth .				2			1	1	This borough is now in the family of the Carters. The electors will again, it is apprehended, choose Sir H[arry] Featherstone They choose Mr. Erskine on the recommendation of the present government to whom they are inclined in general to give one, and it is apprehended, with civility and proper application at the moment preceeding, they might be

ENGLISH BOROUGHS, CLOSE—*continued.*

	Pro.	Hopeful.	Doubtful.	Con.	Pro.	Hopeful.	Doubtful.	Con.	
									prevailed on to elect a steady friend of the administration, which Mr. Erskine can't be classed. It is therefore classed 1 *doubtful*, 1 *con*, as Sir Harry Featherstone would be.
Newport, Isle of Wight	1			1	2				This borough has always been manageable through the government of the Isle of Wight and the inhabitants of that island. Sir Richard Worsley will, it is apprehended, still retain one seat there and be *pro*. The other vice Mr. John St. John, with small attention but some address, may, it is apprehended, be secured by administration.
Yarmouth, Hants			2		2				On nearly the same interest as Newport when drawing together, but now believed entirely in the Holmes interest and will require great *attention and management*, but with that both seats will most probably be had. N B. Jervois Clarke.
Newton, Hants .	2				2				Mr. Barrington will be elected again undoubtedly if he chooses it, but this borough being under an agreement between his family and Sir Richard Worsley there is little doubt but that a seat may be got from Sir Richard. Both therefore classed *pro*.
Lymington . .			1		1	2			This borough is Sir H[arry] Burrard's. Mr. Burrard, an officer of service in America, Sir Harry's nephew and heir, has grievances in the army, at least Sir Harry used and lately has made complaint for him.

ENGLISH BOROUGHS, CLOSE—*continued.*

	Pro.	Hopeful.	Doubtful.	Con	Pro.	Hopeful.	Doubtful.	Con.	
Christ Church .		1	1			2			Sir Harry was always attached to government, and his nephew, notwithstanding complaints, goes with administration. He will, it is apprehended, so continue, with civility and conversation with his uncle and him. Mr. Gibbon certainly is connected with Lord Loughborough, but at present aggrieved and is going abroad. Not likely to come in again, and his seat with attention may be got. Is under the influence of Mr. Hooper, commissioner of the customs, and Sir James Harris, his relation, has some interest also, [so] that most likely the same gentlemen will be re-elected. But if Sir J[ohn] Frederick should not choose to come in again, his father being dead, it is apprehended *two* friends might be got in on talking properly to Mr. Hooper. At present the two members cannot be set down *pro*, but in future it is thought they would be so. At present they are therefore classed hopeful and doubtful and in future both hopeful.
Whitechurch .	2				2				Lord Sidney's borough and will return two friends certainly.
Petersfield . .		1		1	2				Mr. Joliffe's borough. Both brothers may again be returned or a friend, it is probable, got in and Mr. William Jolliffe with management made *steady*.
Tamworth . .	1			1	1			1	Is Lord Townshend's and Lord Weymouth's borough. One classed for and one at present

ENGLISH BOROUGHS, CLOSE—*continued.*

	Pro	Hopeful	Doubtful	Con.	Pro	Hopeful	Doubtful	Con.	
									against and classed so hereafter, but probably with attention may not be so entirely *con.*
Newcastle-under-Lime	2				2				Lord Gower's and will return, it is apprehended, two friends.
Dunwich	1			1	1			1	This borough is between the two present members who will be returned again and, it is apprehended, stand as classed.
Orford				2			2		Lord Hertford's borough ; will not be altered probably, but yet only classed doubtful, as the family like to support.
Eye	2				2				Lord Cornwallis's, who, it is apprehended, will bring in two friends.
Gatton		1	1			2			Lord Newhaven's. Both, it is apprehended, may be got with *attention.*
Haselmere	2				2				Sir James Lowther's borough, who, it is apprehended, will bring in two friends.
Bletchingley	1	1					1	1	Sir Robert Clayton's. Although Mr. Kenrick may be well inclined, yet at present he must only be reckoned hopeful in case of a change, and it is not certain he will again come in, therefore *doubtful.*
Reigate, Surry		2			2				The Yorks and Sir Charles Cocks. The present members will probably be elected or persons equally hopeful.
Horsham				2	2				Is Lady Irwin's borough ; has generally been got for the friends of government by attention and may probably be so again, but it will require now a little more management
Bramber			1	1	1	1			This borough is divided between the Duke of Rutland and Sir H[enry] Gough. Sir Henry

ENGLISH BOROUGHS, CLOSE—*continued.*

	Pro.	Hopeful.	Doubtful.	Con.	Pro.	Hopeful.	Doubtful.	Con.	
Midhurst . .		1		1	2				Gough will come in again; Major Stanhope is against, but on a future event it is apprehended that the Duke of Rutland will bring in a steady friend, and Sir Henry Gough is in inclination generally with government. This borough is Lord Montague's, and with civility and attention may be got to return two friends.
East Grinstead .				2			2		Is Lord Sackville's. His friends were in opposition to the present administration, have changed on some negotiation lately, were against the Bill, but in a future event might not be so perhaps, and therefore are classed as doubtful.
Steyning . .				2			2		This belongs to Sir John Honeywood. His uncle, the member for Kent, was against the East India Bill; is apprehended to be rather averse to the present administration, though brought in the present members for this place from friendship and attachment to the Rockinghams. It is likely Sir John would himself come in in future, and it is probable with management and civility he might bring in a steady friend if an agreeable person could be pitched upon.
Appleby . .	1			1	1			1	Sir James Lowther and Lord Thanet and probably will be the same again.
Droitwich .				2				2	Lord Foley's family; the same again probably, and will stand as classed.

ENGLISH BOROUGHS, CLOSE—*continued.*

	Pro.	Hopeful.	Doubtful.	Con.	Pro.	Hopeful.	Doubtful.	Con.	
Bewdley .				1				1	Lord Westcote's, and will come in again.
Marlborough	1	1			2				This place is under Lord Aylesbury's influence. Lord Courtown, it is apprehended, would be clearly *for* Mr. Woodley seldom attends and still seldomer votes He is said to hold the seat only temporarily and occasionally ; therefore it is apprehended in future both seats may be classed for.
Calne . . .	2				2				Lord Shelburne's recommendation ; probably the present members will be reelected, but if not friends who will equally act with.
Malmsbury .			1	1	2				This borough was in proper hands that gave no trouble but received the recommendations made. It is not known with certainty how it exactly stands in this respect now, but it is apprehended it may be revived and therefore classed both for. Mr. Calvert, junior, would not be against it is supposed on an event.
Old Sarum . .	2				2				Mr Thomas Pitt's. The same or two friends.
Heytesbury . .	1			1	1			1	This borough is divided between the Duke of Marlborough and Mr. Acourt. The same members will probably be reelected and stand as they do, unless Mr. Acourt by civility may be made steady.
Westbury . .	2				2				Lord Abingdon's ; probably the same members will be reelected or friends
Luggershall .	1			1	2				Mr. Selwyn's borough ; will come in himself. Attention will

ENGLISH BOROUGHS, CLOSE—*continued*.

	Pro.	Hopeful.	Doubtful.	Con.	Pro.	Hopeful.	Doubtful.	Con.	
									obtain his return of another friend.
Wilton	2				2				Lord Pembroke's. Probably the same members or a friend in the room of Mr. Hamilton.
Downton . .				2	2				Mr. Shaftoe's borough. He will come in again himself. Attention and civility may probably obtain the other seat.
Great Bedwin .				2	2				Lord Aylesbury's. Mr. Methuen may probably be again returned. Sir M[errick] Burrell perhaps not wish it, and therefore with civility Lord Aylesbury may probably be prevailed on to return *another friend*.
[Total Close Boroughs]	49	34	18	76	99	32	15	31	

WALES.

	Pro.	Hopeful.	Doubtful.	Con.	Pro.	Hopeful.	Doubtful.	Con.	
Anglesea . .	1				1				The same again.
Beaumaris . .	1				1				The same again.
Brecon . .			1				1		The same again. Mr. Morgan and his family wish in general to support government and go one way always. Their relationship and connection with Sir Charles Gould, who holds so beneficial an office under government, draws them more strongly to these sentiments, and, although they voted for the East India Bill, yet perhaps would not go through in other questions, and this connection in future might with some others be used to good

WALES—*continued*

	Pro.	Hopeful	Doubtful	Con	Pro.	Hopeful	Doubtful	Con.	
									effect, it is thought They are in future classed hopeful.
Brecon Town			1		1				The same member. Vide remark above. Classed only hopeful as the Morgan's, but thought would be *for* in future
Cardiff . . .	1				1				Lord Mountstewart has the influence here. It is said that he will not bring Sir H[erbert] Mackworth in again. His Lordship has had negotiations, it is said, with the present ministers. It will be seen what part he will take in the House of Lords, but it is thought not too much in his situation to class the person his Lordship shall bring in as *hopeful.*
Cardiganshire .	1				1				Lord Lisburne will most likely come in again. He feels himself to have been neglected by Lord North having had no notice taken of him and does not attend. His brother, the general, is kept by the expectations given him of the government of Canada, or, some say, the lieutenant government of Gibraltar and votes with administration, and it seems best here to state the whole connection, as Lord Lisburne is certainly worth attending to Besides his brother, there is his brother-in-law, Mr. Shaftoe, who has the borough of Downton, who probably also might be made favourable, and if he did not bring in another friend would probably with attention and management accept a

WALES—*continued*

	Pro.	Hopeful.	Doubtful.	Con.	Pro	Hopeful	Doubtful	Con.	
									recommendation Thus this family would be 4 votes
·Cardigan		1			1				Mr. John Campbell ; is much inclined to support government, and it is thought might throughout be classed hopeful ; was once strongly attached to Lord North. If he should desire to again stand for this place, might come, but had views on Pembrokeshire and has a good interest in Scotland for the shire of Nairn which elects at the next election.
·Carmarthenshire			1				1		Most probably the same again, for young Mr. Rice will scarce enter into a contest at present for the county, but probably if he wishes now to come into Parliament will come in for Carmarthen Town.
·Carmarthen .			1			1			Mr. George Phillips probably again ; if not, perhaps young Mr. Rice ; vide remark above ; in either case *hopeful.* Mr. Phillips is a relation of Mr. *Clayton* of *Marlow.*
Caernarvonshire	1				1				Under the circumstance of Lord Newborough's family, most likely Mr. Parry will come in again. He was connected with Lord Bulkeley, and therefore is classed *for.*
·Caernarvon Town				1	1				Mr. Glyn Wyn votes with *now, having office,* but in a future parliament, as it is apprehended he will come in again, he most likely will be *pro.*
Denbigh .		1					1		Same again. Attends very little but may be *hopeful*
Denbighshire .	1						1		Sir Watkins Williams Wynn again.

WALES—*continued*

	Pro.	Hopeful	Doubtful	Con.	Pro.	Hopeful	Doubtful	Con.	
Flintshire			1					1	Same again; connected with Lord Fitzwilliam Etc.
Flint Town	1				1				Same again; apprehended to go as Sir Watkin.
Glamorganshire		1					1		Same again; thought doubtful.
Haverfordwest				1		1			Same again. Against now but may with civility perhaps be classed hopeful. He was entangled with some securities to the customs.
Merionethshire			1					1	Probably the same gentleman again, very doubtful how he may act and therefore classed con.
Montgomeryshire			1					1	He perhaps may come in again, although not clearly so; a good deal depends on Lord Powis, who was not satisfied with his conduct but did not oppose him at the last general election. What may be Lord Powis's sentiments now, without communication, can't be known, but Lady Powis having a pension makes it easier to converse with Lord Powis.
Montgomery Town			1					1	How far Lord Powis may be engaged to bring Mr. Keene in again can't be ascertained without talking with his Lordship on it, and this cannot be done until the moment; therefore classed con.
Pembrokeshire				1		1			Sir Hugh Owen again, who on being talked with as well as his cousin, though now *perhaps against*, it is hoped might be *pro*. Mr. Hugh Owen has grievances, and indeed some fair ones.
Pembroke Town				1		1			Mr. Hugh Owen again; included in the last preceding remark.

H

WALES—*continued.*

	Pro.	Hopeful.	Doubtful.	Con.	Pro.	Hopeful.	Doubtful.	Con	
Radnorshire .				1	1				Mr. Johnes again ; in office now, *against* ; in future *pro* ; it is thought most agreeable to *his* *sentiments.*
Radnor Town .				1	1				Mr. Lewis or his son will most probably come in again ; now against ; thought with civility and conversation would in future be *pro.*
[Total Wales] .	5	4	4	11	8	10	2	4	

SCOTLAND.

	Pro.	Hopeful.	Doubtful.	Con.	Pro.	Hopeful.	Doubtful.	Con	
Aberdeenshire .	1				1				If Mr. Garden wishes to come in again it is apprehended he may, but at his age it is a question ; attached to Mr. Dundas, who can best tell what would happen if Mr. Garden should decline.
Aberbrothock .		1			1				If Mr. Adam Drummond should come in again he would be *pro* it is apprehended. His attachment to Lord North made him go for the East India Bill though averse to it. If he should not come in probably Sir David Carnegie would, and it is thought he would be favourable in either case, therefore *pro.*
Airshire . . .	1				1				It is hoped Sir Adam Ferguson may come in again, but there may be a contest unless it is prevented.
Argyleshire . .				1	1				Lord Frederick Campbell will undoubtedly come in again ; may vote *con* now, but on a change, it is apprehended, would be pro.

SCOTLAND—*continued.*

	Pro.	Hopeful.	Doubtful.	Con.	Pro.	Hopeful.	Doubtful.	Con.	
Bamfshire . .			1		1				Lord Fife will come in again; he is not a great attender but was formerly attached to Mr. Grenville; he varies and is uncertain without explanation, and therefore he is classed *doubtful*, although he may be more steady. Mr. Dundas says *pro.*
Berwickshire .	1				1				It is hoped Mr. Scott may come in again and that he will be *pro* in both situations. Scott will be turned out, but a friend of Mr. Dundas's will come in.
Caithness alternate with Bute			1				1		Does not return a member this time, but . . . Will probably be one of the Bute family, either James Wortley Montague Stuart or perhaps Colonel Charles Stuart. Vide remark on this family under Cardiff, who with civility and address may, it is thought, be all secured. 1 peer, 3 commons.
Anstruther, Wester, Etc.			1		1				Mr. Anstruther at present takes the line of support of government because he holds an office, but if a change, in a future parliament, would, it is believed, support as he does now.
Culross, Etc., Etc.			1		1				Major Campbell. If again elected, it is apprehended would follow as remarked in the last observation.
Coupar, Etc. .			1				1		If elected again, will be against as now, but this depends much on government and Mr. Dundas. (An opposition probable from Captain Laird who, if he comes in, will be *pro.*) [1]

[1] The sentences in parenthesis were inserted in smaller script, apparently after the original paper was prepared, or at least so appear in the transcript.

SCOTLAND—*continued.*

	Pro.	Hopeful	Doubtful	Con.	Pro.	Hopeful	Doubtful	Con.	
Dumbartonshire				1	1				Will probably come in and be *against.* (Mr. Dundas thinks he will certainly be turned out and a friend brought in.) [1]
Dumbarton, Etc.				1	1				As the last if he is let come in. Query, Mr. Dundas, same as above.
Dumfriesshire .			1		1				Sir Robert Laurie will probably come in again. His conduct will in a good measure, though perhaps not entirely, depend on the Duke of Queensbury. His inclination is to be with government. He may from the Duke be at present against, but on any change or future parliament it is apprehended would be both *pro.*
Dumfries, Etc. .			1		1				Whether Sir Robert Herries will again be returned depends much on who has the return of the borough. Mr. Dundas can judge of this. If Sir Robert Herries is again returned, although at present he may be doubtful, it is thought that he would be for. If he is not returned it is then supposed the Duke if Queensbury will return a person who shall be *pro.* (Mr. Dundas thinks Governor Johnstone or Peter Millar, banker in Edinburgh.) [1]
Edinburghshire .	1				1				Mr. Dundas as before.
Edinburgh Town			1		1				Mr. Dundas must say what will arise here or whether if Blair again comes in he can be made better than doubtful. Mr. -

---

[1] The sentences in parenthesis were inserted in smaller script, apparently after the original paper was prepared, or at least so appear in the transcript.

Scotland—*continued.*

	Pro.	Hopeful.	Doubtful.	Con.	Pro.	Hopeful.	Doubtful.	Con.	
Elginshire . .				1	1				Dundas says *pro* or he will not come in. Lord William Gordon will certainly come in again. He acts at present and with propriety with the present administration, and he has obtained for a friend of theirs the late seat at Horsham But it is apprehended there are hopes that in a future parliament, holding the offices he does, he would be *pro*, and it may reasonably be expected that he would give his assistance with attention to get the seats at Horsham.
Fifeshire .				1	1				If Skeene comes in again he will, it is thought, be *for*, and very properly following government. If not, an opposition may easily be given him.
Forfarshire . .	1				1				Will, it is apprehended, come in again and be steadily *for*. (Will probably bring in a friend and stand for Roxburghshire).[1]
Haddingtonshire	1				1				Most likely come in again and will be *for*.
Invernessshire .			1		1				It is apprehended Mr Fraser will not come in but some friend or connection of the Duke of Gordon who, it is hoped, will be for. Mr. Dundas thinks he will undoubtedly be turned out and a friend brought in.
Inverness, Etc				1	1				Sir Hector Monro will, it is apprehended, come in again He may be doubtful in the present, but in future *pro*.

[1] The sentences in parenthesis were inserted in smaller script, apparently after the original paper was prepared, or at least so appear in the transcript.

SCOTLAND—*continued.*

	Pro.	Hopeful.	Doubtful.	Con.	Pro.	Hopeful.	Doubtful.	Con.	
Irvine, Etc. . .				1	1				Sir Archibald Edmonstone will probably come in for these boroughs again unless there happens to be some agreement with the Bute family for the next turn. Sir Archibald very properly *votes now* with the present government but would undoubtedly so, as properly, with the next in a future administration.
Kincardinshire .		1			1				Lord Adam Gordon will, it is apprehended, come in again and be *pro.*
Kinross (not now but Clackmanan)			1	•	1				Whether Sir Thomas Dundas will be able to carry Clackmanan cannot now be said, as papers cannot be got at ; it is therefore put doubtful. Mr. Dundas says either Colonel Abercrombie or Mr. Erskine of Alloa will come in and be *pro.*
Kintore, Etc. .				1	1				General Morris will come in again, it is apprehended, or Mr. Dundas says General Grant and in a future parliament with.
Kirkcudbright .			1		1				If Mr. Johnstone should come in again it is hoped he will be *pro.* If he does not, Mr. Gordon or a friend of Lord Galloway's may and would be *pro.* Or, Mr. Dundas says, probably Richard Oswald.
Kirkaldy, Etc. .		1			1				Sir John Henderson will, it is thought, come in again and be *pro.*
Lanerkshire . .		1			1				Mr. A[ndrew] Stuart, it is apprehended, will be returned again and be *pro,* as the Duke of Hamilton wishes probably not Mr. Stuart but another friend.

Scotland—*continued*.

	Pro.	Hopeful	Doubtful.	Con	Pro	Hopeful	Doubtful	Con.	
Lander . . .				1	1				If Mr. Charteris comes in again, which Mr. Dundas can best say, he will be *con* If Mr. Colt shall succeed he will be *pro.* Mr Dundas says if Mr. Charteris comes in he must be *pro.*
Linlithgowshire .				1	1				Sir William Cunningham is at present warm in support of the administration. If he comes in he may not be quite steady, though most probably will be so, because he leans to Lord Mountstuart Etc and affects to go as that family does ; but a word from Lord Hoptoun might set this right both *now* and in *future*.
Cromarty Query, alternate with Nairn	1							1	As papers cannot be got at it is put doubtful, referring to Mr. Dundas to class. Query, Mr. J. Campbell of Calder.
Orkney, Etc .				1				1	Canvassed in both cases *con*, because uncertain But Mr. Dundas will say and best knows what is become of Mr. Baikie and what chance he has
Peebleshire . .			1		1				It is not recollected, nor by the Calendar does it appear, who came in in the room of Mr. Murray. The interest here is the Duke of Queensberry's. It is hoped that he will be with, and therefore in a future parliament this place is canvassed for.
Perthshire . .				1	1				General Murray, it is apprehended, will be returned again and with government in a future parliament as he is now.
Renfrewshire .		1			1				Mr. Macdowal is just come into parliament, Shaw Stewart having quitted on an agreement.

SCOTLAND—*continued.*

	Pro.	Hopeful	Doubtful	Con.	Pro.	Hopeful	Doubtful	Con.	
									To what extent this go or whether to a future parliament it is not yet known. It will be endeavoured to come at this. If Mr. Macdowal continues it is hoped he may be *pro.* If Mr. Shaw Stewart comes in he will be *con.*
Ross-shire . .			1		1				As the chief of the Mackenzie's, brother and heir to the late Colonel Humberstone, is deaf and dumb, it is unlikely he will think of coming into parliament, and therefore it is most likely that Lord Macleod will be elected again, and he will be *pro.*
Roxburghshire				1	1				It may be doubted whether Sir Gilbert Elliot will be again reelected. If he is not, but a friend of the Duke of Roxburgh's should succeed, it is apprehended that he may be *pro,* although Sir Gilbert will be *con.* This is therefore classed doubtful. Mr. Dundas says he will certainly be turned out and perhaps Mr. Douglas of Douglas be elected.
Selkirkshire . .		1			1				Mr. Pringle will most likely come in again and be *for.*
Selkirk . .				1	1				It is apprehended Sir James Cockburn will not come in again but that some friend agreeable to the Duke of Buccleugh, the Duke of Queensbury, Etc., will come in and be *pro.* Sir James Cockburn is out by agreement.
Stirlingshire . .				1				1	Whether Sir Thomas Dundas will be able to support his seat here is uncertain. If he is, he must

SCOTLAND—*continued.*

	Pro.	Hopeful	Doubtful	Con.	Pro.	Hopeful	Doubtful	Con.	
									probably bring in Lord Graham elsewhere, as last time, therefore in this uncertainty this place is classed *doubtful*.
Stranraer, Etc. .				1	1				It is apprehended these boroughs will the next parliament be under the influence of the Galloways. If so a friend will come in and be *pro*. But whether in the Galloway family or not, Mr. Adam does not seem likely to succeed; perhaps Lord Dalrymple, who is in public service abroad, should Lord Stair have this next turn.
Sutherlandshire .				1	1				Mr. Weemys will come in again, or perhaps his son if [of] age, and either will be *pro*.
Wigtounshire	1				1				Mr. Keith Stewart will certainly come in again and be *pro*.
Wick, Etc. . .			1				1		Mr. Ross will scarce come in again, it is apprehended. These are a parcel of very compound boroughs. They are classed doubtful, and Mr. Dundas can best say whether good can be drawn out of them. Mr. Dundas thinks General Ross will not get in and that there is a chance of getting in a friend.
[Total Scotland]	7	7	10	21	40	2	2	1	

1783, December 15.—Richard Atkinson to John Robinson. Endorsed by Robinson: "Answered immediately, and went accordingly." "The Lord Advocate wishes to get an appointment made for you and he and Mr. Pitt and myself to meet as soon as possible, in the most secret way, not from any improper desire of secrecy but lest the measure in agitation should be guessed at if an interview was known. It has ended in appointing this evening at seven o'clock at the Advocate's house in Leicester Fields, when he will have some dinner for us. . . . I understand in general that all goes right."

The following memoranda are endorsed on the back by Robinson : " Parliamentary State of boroughs and situations, with remarks, preparatory to a new parliament in 178[3 ?] on a change of administration and Mr. Pitt's coming in, sketched out at several meetings at Lord Advocate Dundas's in Leicester Square, and a wild wide calculate of the money wanted for seats, but which I always disapproved and thought very wrong."

From internal evidence and the above letter from Richard Atkinson to Robinson, it is probable that this paper was prepared in the period from December 15 to December 31, 1783.

FRIENDS—CLOSE, OR UNDER DECISIVE INFLUENCE

Sir James Lowther	9	Cockermouth	2
		Appleby.	1
		Haslemere	2
		Carlisle	1
		Cumberland.	1
		Westmoreland	2
Earl Temple	3	Buckingham	2
		Buckinghamshire	1
Earl of Shelburne	3	Wycomb	1
		Calne	2
Lord Weymouth	3	Weobly	2
		Tamworth	1
Duke of Bridgewater	2	Brackley	2
Lord Sydney	1	Whitechurch	1
Lord Gower	3	Newcastle	2
		Litchfield	1
Lord Cornwallis	2	Eye	2
The Yorkes	3	Ryegate	2
		Cambridgeshire	1
Duke of Rutland	2	Bramber	1
		Scarborough	1
Mr. T[homas] Pitt	2	Old Sarum	2
Lord Abingdon	2	Westbury	2
Lord Pembroke	2	Wilton	2
Government influence	4	Saltash	2
		Queensborough	2

FOR COMMUNICATION.

These are supposed to be partly accessible in one way and part in other ways, which till communication cannot be well judged of.

Duke of Northumberland	7	Launceston . . .	2 ⎫
		Newport	2 ⎪
		Beeralston . . .	2 ⎬
		Northumberland	1 ⎭
Mr. Elliot	7	Liskeard . .	2 ⎫
		St. Germans	2 ⎪ Suppose
		Grampound	2 ⎬ 10,000l.
		Cornwall . .	1 ⎭
Lord Falmouth .	3	Tregony	2 ⎫ 9,000l.
		Mitchell . . .	1 ⎭
Sir F[rancis] Bassett . .	5	Mitchell	1 ⎫
		Truro (Quere) .	2 ⎬ 12,000l.
		Penryn (Quere) . .	2 ⎭
Lord Orford	4	Ashburton .	1 ⎫
		Callington (Quere)	2 ⎬
		Castle Rising .	1 ⎭
Duke of Newcastle . .	6	Aldborough	2 ⎫
		Boroughbridge . .	2 ⎪
		Retford . . .	1 ⎬
		Newark . . .	1 ⎭
Lord Sandwich . . .	3	Huntingdon .	2 ⎫ Suppose office
		Huntingdonshire	1 ⎭
Mr. Howard (Bagot) .	1	Castle Rising . .	1
Mr. Hooper	2	Christchurch . .	2
Lord Hertford . .	3	Orford	2 ⎫ Suppose office
		Coventry. . . .	1 ⎭
Lord Sackville . .	2	East Grinstead . .	2
Sir John Honeywood .	2	Steyning	1
		And himself . . .	1
Lord Aylesbury . .	4	Marlborough. . .	2 ⎫ Suppose 1 seat
		Great Bedwin . .	2 ⎭ 3,000l.
Mr. Selwyn . . .	2	Luggershall . . .	1 ⎫ Ditto 3,500l.
		And himself . .	1 ⎭
Mr. Shaftoe .	2	Downton	1 ⎫ Ditto 3,500l.
		And himself . . .	1 ⎭
Lord Lisburne	2	Cardiganshire . .	1
		Berwick	1
Fonnereau and Crespigny	2	Aldborough, Suffolk	2
Government Influence .	3	Portsmouth . .	1 ⎫
		And Sir H. Feather-		
		stone	1 ⎪ Arrangement
		Dartmouth . . .	1 ⎬ rather than
		And Mr. Holdsworth	1 ⎪ expence.
		Harwich	1 ⎪
		And Mr. Robinson .	1 ⎪
		Plymouth . . .	1 ⎭

Lord Powis	2	Montgomery	1
		Ludlow	1
Lord Galway	2	Pomfret	2
Mr. Walsh			
Duke of Chandos	1	Winchester	1

Money.

Earl Verney	2	Wendover	2	Suppose for 7,000l.
Lord Edgecumbe	6	Lostwithiel	2	
		Bossiney	1	18,000l.
		Fowey	1	
		Plympton	2	
Mr. Buller, junior	2	West Loo	2	6,000l.
Mr. Phillips	2	Camelford	2	8,000l.
Mr. Steward	4	Weymouth	3	9,000l.
		And himself	1	
Mr. Lucas	2	Wareham	2	6,000l.
Sir T. Frankland	2	Thirsk	2	7,000l.
Mr. Praed	1	St. Ives	1	3,500l.
Mr. Luttrell	2	Minehead	1	Probably Beaufoy
		And himself	1	
Sir R. Worsley	2	Newton	1	2,000l.
		Newport, Hants	1	Himself probably
Mr. Holmes	3	Newport	1	9,000l.
		Yarmouth	2	
Sir H. Burrard	2	Lymington	1	Suppose 2 seats
		And his nephew	1	6,000l.
Lord Newhaven	2	Gatton	2	8,000l.
Lady Irwin	2	Horsham	2	7,000l.
Lord Montague	2	Midhurst	1	4,000l.
		And Mr. Drummond	1	
Government Influence	13	Malmsbury	2	Annual. The election year somewhat extra.
		Hastings	2	5,000l.
		Rye	2	3,000l.
		Seaford	2	4,000l.
		Sandwich	2	2,000l
		Hythe	2	2,000l.
		Scarborough	1	1,000l.
		Winchelsea	2	
Sir Edward Deering	2	New Romney	1	
		Himself	1	

No Money.

Messrs. Drake	2	Agmondesham	2
Mr. Buller, senior	2	East Looe	2
Duke of Bedford	3	Okehampton	1
		Tavistock	2

Lord Spencer .	3	Okehampton	1
		St. Albans .	1
		Northampton (Quere) .	1
Duke of Marlborough .	5	Woodstock . . .	2
		Oxford .	1
		Oxfordshire .	1
		Heytesbury . .	1
Sir R. Clayton	2	Bletchinglye . . .	2
Mr. Jolliffe	2	Petersfield	2
		Probably his brother.	
Lord Westmoreland	2	Lyme	2
Mr. Lawrence .	2	Ripon	2
Mr. Leigh .	2	Newton, Lancaster	2
Duke of Grafton	2	Thetford	2

ADVERSE.

Duke of Devonshire	4	Knaresborough . . .	2
		Derbyshire	1
		Derby	1
Lord Fitzwilliam .	3	Malton	2
		Higham Ferrars . . .	1
Sir T[homas] Dundas . . .	3	Richmond	2
		Orkney . . .	1
Lord Townsend	1	Tamworth . . .	1
Lord Foley . . .	3	Droitwich	2
		Worcestershire	1
Mr. Lister	2	Clitheroe	2
Lord Carlisle	2	Morpeth .	2
Lord North	1	Banbury . . .	1
Sir H[arry] Featherstone . . .	1	Portsmouth	1

OPEN BOROUGHS WHERE SEATS MAY PROBABLY BE OBTAINED WITH EXPENCE.

Aylesbury	1	Suppose . . .	2,500l.
Totness . . .	1	Suppose . . .	3,000l.
Hedon . . .	1	Suppose	2,000l.
Grimsby . . .	1	Suppose	2,000l.
Ilchester	1	Suppose . . .	2,500l.
Milborn Port . .	1	Suppose	3,000l.
Stockbridge . . .	2	Suppose	6,000l.
Stafford	1	Suppose . . .	2,000l.
Arundel	1	Suppose . . .	3,000l.
Hindon	1	Suppose . .	3,000l.
Wooton Bassett . . .	1	Suppose . . .	3,000l.
Honiton . . .	1	Suppose	3,000l.
Poole .	1		
Devizes	2		
Chippenham	1		

To these may be added *Westminster, York, Gloucester*, Bristol (if Mr Burke should stand), and other places in which contests may arise where administration may see fit to take a part.

ABSTRACT.

Communication .	41,000*l.*
Money . .	117,500*l.*
Open	35,000*l.*
	193,500*l.*

Besides arrangements with the Duke of Northumberland, Lord Orford, The Duke of Newcastle, Mr. Howard, Mr Hooper, Lord Sackville, Sir John Honeywood.

PRIVATE MEMORANDUMS AND GENERAL REMARKS.[1]

st Class

Those places classed under friends, or close, under decisive influence, have been sufficiently explained so as to show how applications are to be made about them But besides the places classed in the extracts under this head there are the following places which are close as to one or both members as follows, marked for communication.

nd Class, which will require some attention, although not so particular an attention as those first classed, and the returns from these places may be expected as follows

These are pretty much in the same situation and will depend upon arrangements and conversations, to be had chiefly by Mr. Pitt, except where he has already minuted some other persons, as first to break the ground at the time he shall appoint Query, The Duke of Northumberland's office. Query, Whether it might not be adviseable for a certain personage to see both the Duke of Northumberland and the Duke of Newcastle, both classed under this head.

rd Class

Money. Of these, Mr. Pitt will consider and determine what is to be done as to Wendover 2, Gatton 2, Thirsk 2, which boroughs are more likely than any others to fall into the hands of his opponents.

---

[1] The title is Robinson's. This paper is explanatory of and supplementary to that framed at the conferences at the house of Dundas, mentioned above. The date of this document would seem to fall, therefore, after December 15, 1783, and parts of its contents seem to indicate that it was prepared previous to the accession of Pitt's administration to office, December 18, 1783.

Scarborough 1.—Mr. P[itt] to converse with the Duke of Rutland upon this, then a joint declaration for the persons fixed on will be proper ; in the meantime Mr R[obinson] will inquire a little how the present state of the borough is since the operation of the disfranchising bill.

Horsham 2.—Lady Irwin's through Lord William Gordon.

Lord Edgecumbe's six seats Mr. P[itt] seemed to think he was in a proper train to get

West Looe 2 seats, Minehead 1, Newton, Hants. 1 : These places Mr. Rose [1] Etc. will be [able] to take care of through Mr. Buller, Mr. Lutterell, Sir Richard Worsley, and Mr Holmes of the Isle of Wight immediately on the change.[2]

Midhurst 2 seats —Probably taken again by the present representatives if agreeable it should be so. If no better channell, Mr. R[obinson] can talk with Lord Montague.

Camelford 2, Weymouth 3, Wareham 2, St Ives 1, Lymington 1, Malmesbury 2, Hastings 2, Rye 2, Seaford 1, Winchelsea 1 : These places to be taken care of by Mr. Rose, etc. having letters prepared to the proper persons to be seen and sent for, the letters to be sent away to those at a distance the moment of the change, so as to have them up immediately in order to arrange and settle matters with them and return them back to their boroughs previous to the dissolution

Hythe 2 —Sir Charles Farnaby and Mr. William Evelyn to be seen and talked to on this at the moment after the change.

Sandwich 2 —Mr. Stephens to be spoke to at the proper moment to arrange this for himself and Mr. Brett

- No Money. Will depend entirely on arrangement and 4th Class. the conversations Mr. Pitt or some other persons of consequence must have with such of this class as are accessible, except Mr. Jolliffe, who Mr. R[obinson] can well undertake to converse with.

[1] George Rose, who became under Pitt Secretary to the Treasury, the position held under North for so long by Robinson.

[2] The " change " repeatedly referred to is apparently the projected dismissal of the coalition ministry of Fox and North and the accession to power of Pitt and those who were working for the defeat of the East India Bill in the House of Lords.

5th Class.   Adverse. To be now considered as impossible to get anything from, yet open to future events.

6th Class.   Open boroughs, where seats may probably be obtained with expence

Aylesbury 2 —Query, Whether better can be had than the old members. This must be considered by Mr Pitt on conversation with Lord Temple, and when the resolution is taken Mr. R[obinson] to send to Mr Bacon.

Honiton 1.—Send Mr. R[obinson] to see Mr. Bacon on this also, for on Mr. Bacon's sending for the proper person *in due time* (and for this it will take double time) will depend on bringing in a friend not in opposition to but with Sir George Yonge and make both come easy.

Hedon 1.—This to be attended to by sending to Mr. Chaytor in due time and having the proper manager up to town at the moment after the change.

Devizes 2 —Mr. Garth must be talked to about this at the proper moment.

Chippenham 1.—See Sir Edward Bayntun on this. Query, Channell through Lord Weymouth.

Poole 1 —Send up for Mr. Lister on the *change* to talk to him. Query, Gulston again if he is able to undertake it as the best man.

Totnes 1.—Mr. Rose to speak to Judge Buller

Grimbsy 1 —A very uncertain seat, but something may turn out on a conversation Mr. Rose should have with Mr. Eyre, the present member, immediately after the change

Stockbridge 2 —There is a chance of getting these two seats, as it is said the last scores have not been well rubbed off. Mr Harmood being talked to by Mr. Rose immediately after the change, it will appear what ground can be made.

Ilchester 1, Milborne Port 1.—These two places to be attended to by Mr. Rose Etc by sending for the proper persons to be on the spot as before stated at the moment of change

Stafford 1 or 2.—Inquiry to be made by Mr. Rose of Loyd of Grey's Inn how this borough now stands. Richard Whitworth might be useful, but quere.

Arundel 1, perhaps two if wanted.—Mr. Fitzherbert, the

present member, if he would come in again, would be the properest person to secure this again either for 1 or both seats, if both should be wished and paid for, and he would do it on the easiest terms by having him and the proper agent up at the moment of change

Hindon 1, or perhaps 2 —Very much as Arundel. Mr Kenyon should be spoke to about this, but if he can't trace out the channel, the proper agent should be sent to immediately on the change if it is wished to have this place secured.

Wooton Bassett 1.—Mr. Strahan purchased the last time ; probably would again this and has the fairest claim on General St. John, through whom by another agent on the spot this borough is always managed. Strahan has always been, and it is believed always would be steady, but should not he be thought proper to be fixed upon to secure the place, there may be much difficulty to get a seat from the St John family, who may want another seat for themselves.

1783, December 29.—George Rose to John Robinson.   Endorsed : "R[eceived] by messenger 9 P.M. and answered immediately. ' J. R." "Monday evening ½ past 6. I send you herewith Mr. Dundas's India Bill of last year, Mr. Fox's Bill with the amendments as it was sent up to the Lords, and his other Bill for the better management of the Territories, Revenues and Commerce of India, which are the three you desired to have

"I will take the proper precautions about the Sheriffs ; and you shall have the canvass corrected in a few days.

"The Chancellor has not been in town yet since I saw you, but I shall be with him tomorrow morning and will take care of Lord Abergavenny's friend in the Commission of Bankrupts. In the meantime your letter to him will prevent his being excluded

"Mr. Philips dines with his two friends today and will arrange matters with them provisionally."

The following memoranda were probably made about the time of the dissolution of parliament, March 25, 1784. Their date is certainly not earlier than February 14, 1784 (see the item concerning Leicester), and not much later than the date of the

I

dissolution. The paper is endorsed · " Places where may be contests in open boroughs and Cinque Ports."

Bedford	. Whitbread Wake	Mr. Steele [1] to speak to Sir William Wake, Mr. Phipps, and Mr. Townsend to get Wake reelected. N.B. Early notice to be given.
Abingdon . .	Loveden	Mr. Rose to speak to Mr. Burton if Loveden declines. Mr. Loveden to be spoke to by Mr. Steele. Loveden comes in
Wallingford .	Aubrey Arcedeckne	Mr. Pitt to see Lord Abingdon to learn his sentiments. Mr. Steele to speak to Mr. Aubrey and learn whether he stands again. Mr. Robinson to speak to Francis Sykes (who has been offered it) to know if he will stand. N.B. Arcedeckne declines.
Aylesbury . .	Ord Bacon	Mr. Rose to learn Lord Temple's wishes and intentions. Quere, What directions Mr. Ord has left. Mr. Robinson to speak to Bacon and learn his intentions.
Marlow . . .	Sir J. B. Warren Clayton	Mr. Steele to learn of Clayton, Mr. Rose of Warren their sentiments and intentions. Mr. Steele to speak to Sir R. Palk to learn of Mr. Vansittart his intentions. Palk married Vansittart's sister.
Cambridge Town	Keene Adeane	Mr. Rose to see Mortlake. *Vice* Keene.
Chester . . .	Bootle T. Grovenor	Quere, vice Bootle.
Truro . .	Gascoigne St. Aubyn	Mr. Pitt to see Lord Falmouth and learn his intentions and the chance of success. Mr. Rose to see Mr. Masterman on the same subject.
Helston . . .	Barwell Lord Hyde	Mr. Rose to see Lord Carmarthen and Mr. Masterman. Mr. Robinson to see Barwell to induce him to stand.
Penryn . . .	Sir F. Bassett Pole Carew	Mr. Rose to concert with Mr. Masterman what can be done and by whom. Supposed one seat may be fought for. Mrs. Herle, Heame, and Colonel Rodd have interest.

[1] Thomas Steele, for seven years after 1783 Rose's colleague as Secretary to the Treasury under Pitt.

Callington . .	Stratton Morshead	Mr. Call says he is to come in. Query, if by Coriton's interest. Mr. Pitt to learn of Lord Orford whether he sets up one or two members and what is to be done ; whether he will let Call in quietly and who is to be second member.
Tiverton. .	Duntze Wilmot	Mr. Rose to learn of Mr. Wilmot the state of things and his own intentions.
Honiton . . .	Yonge Wilkinson	Mr. Steele to learn from Sir G. Collyer whether he has any interest and what and to get rid of him Mr. Atkinson[1] to learn from Macpherson whether he will undertake for , Macleod and to what amount.
Plymouth .	Rogers Darby	Mr. Rose to learn of Masterman what he has done and concert with him what is further to be done. This, *vice* Rogers. Another candidate to be named *vice* Darby.
Totness . . .	Sir P. J. Clark Lancelot Browne	Lord Mulgrave takes care of himself *vice* Browne. Buller has the power. Mr. Rose to follow up a plan he has about the other seat.
Barnstaple . .	Bassett Cleveland	Devaynes to have *early* notice *vice* Bassett.
Bridport. . .	Beckford Scott	Mr. Atkinson to learn of Sam Smith whether his son will stand or not.
Shaftesbury . .	Mortimer Sykes	Mr. Steele to apply through Lord Howe to Mortimer and learn Mortimer's wishes about another candidate.
Poole. .	Morton Pitt Gulston	Mr. Atkinson to converse with F. Baring on this subject. Lister can do a great deal ; Nicholson ; Olive. Mr. Pitt to learn the intentions and views of the family. Mr. Robinson to write to Lister.
Beverley. . .	Pennyman Anderson	Mr. R. Smith to follow up a plan he has in view for his brother-in-law, Mr. Barnard *vice* Anderson.

---

[1] Richard Atkinson, a friend of Robinson and one of the contractors who made profit in the American Revolution, his relations with the government being the subject of a parliamentary investigation. He was active in the negotiations preliminary to the accession of Pitt and in the East India Company, hence his participation in this election.

Wigan	Horace Walpole	
	Cotes	
Leicester. .	Booth Grey	
	Ashby	
Boston . .	Sir P. Burrell	Mr. R. Smith to pursue the plan of getting Turner to stand *vice* Sibthorpe.
	Sibthorpe	
Grimsby .	Eyre	Mr Rose to speak to Mr. Froggatt about a candidate. Clayton's interest will (with money) bring in one. Evelyn Anderson probably commands the other.
	Harrison	
Lincoln .	Viner	R Smith to follow up the plan for his brother. Mr. Rose to find a butcher who has great interest
	Cawthorne	
Westminster	Fox	
	Sir C. Wray	
London .		
Lynn .	Thomas Walpole	Mr. Pitt to see Lord Orford about a member *vice* Walpole.
	C. Molineux	
Yarmouth .	Charles Townshend	Sir J[ohn] Wodehouse joins Townshend.
	Richard Walpole	
Norwich . . .	Sir H. Harbow	Secure.
	Bacon	Wyndham opposes.
Northampton	Lord Lucan	Mr. Robinson to consult H. Drummond about opposing Lord Lucan and to know whether Compton comes in in the place of Rodney Lord Compton comes in. Lord Lucan cannot be shaken.
	G. Rodney	
Newcastle-upon-Tyne	Ridley	.
	Bowes	
Berwick . . .	Delaval	Mr. Rose to concert with the Duke of Northumberland for two candidates.
	Vaughan	
East Retford	Clinton	Mr. Pitt to enquire of the Duke of Newcastle whether anything can be done for the second seat.
	Amcotts	
Nottingham .	R. Smith	Quere, Sir J. B Warren in room of Cooke.
	Cooke	
Bridgnorth .	Pigot	Mr. Rose to speak to Lord Gower.
	Whitmore	
Taunton .	Halliday	
	Hammett	
Ilchester .	S Smith	
	Cust	
Bridgwater .	Acland	Mr. Steele to learn whether Acland will stand again
	Paulett	
Bath .	Pratt	Wanted, a candidate vice Moysey. Quere, Jarret Smith. Mr. Pitt to consult Lord Camden.
	Moysey	

Bristol .	. Daubeny	Mr. Rose to talk to T. Crawford.
	Brickdale	
Stockbridge	. Luttrell	Mr. Robinson to see two friends.
	Luttrell	Mr. Rose to speak to Froggatt.
Southampton	. Sloane	Fleming *vice* Fuller. Wanted,
	Fuller	another candidate.
Stafford .	Sheridan	Mr. Rose to arrange with Lord
	Monckton	Gower an opposition to Sheridan.
Litchfield	. . Anson	Ditto in room of Anson.
	Gilbert	
Ipswich . .	Staunton	Sir W. East and Middleton are to
	Wollaston	stand.
Aldborough,	Fonnereau	Mr. Rose says Crespigny has settled
Suffolk	Crespigny	with Fonnereau that Crespigny
		has power to sell one and come in
		for the other. Mr. Robinson says
		Fonnereau has offered the seat to
		Boehm for 2,500*l.* and 1,200*l.* on
		each change
Sudbury .	Sir P. Blake	Mr. Rose says a seat is secure through
	Sir J. Marriot	Crespigny ; Mr. Robinson says
		there can be no contest more
		insecure. Crespigny says if you
		will not oppose he will come in him-
		self and bring a friend for 1,500*l.*
		Mr. Steele to learn from Sir P. Blake
		his intentions about standing.
Southwark . .	Hotham	Wanted a candidate in room of
	Thornton	Hotham.
Coventry . .	Lord Sheffield	The people have applied that nobody
	· Conway	may be set up, for they mean to
		set up a son of S. Smith of Alder-
		manbury and another by a union
		to turn out the present members.
Worcester .	Rous	*Berwick,* a banker at Worcester, will
	Ward	stand *vice* Rous.
Salisbury	Hussey	Wanted a candidate *vice* Hussey.
	Bouverie	
Devizes .	Sir J. Long	Lublock intends to stand *vice* Jones.
	H. V. Jones	Mr. Robinson to see Harward ;
		Mr. Rose and Nepean ditto.
Chippenham	. Dawkins	Lord Weymouth to be spoke to by
	Fludyer	Mr. Dundas about Sir Edward
		Bayntun's interest. Fludyer to
		be spoke, to concert.
Hindon .	Kenyon	Quere, if Wildman, through the
	Wraxall	Chancellor, can do anything with
		Beckford's interest.
Wootton Bassett	St. John	
	Strahan	

Dover	Heniker	Mr. Rose to speak to Russel, a friend
	Trevanion	of Mr. Pitt by Mr. Prettyman, and
		to Devaynes about Daniel Minet.
Seaford	Durand	Newberry through Chatfield Turner
	D'Oyly	says that Newberry and Newnham
		of Maresfield can come in.
Sandwich	Stephens	Supposed Stephens and Brett
	Sutton	
Hythe	Farnaby	
	Evelyn	
New Romney		
Winchelsea		

1784, March 27—Duke Street, Westminster. George Rose to John Robinson. Endorsed by Robinson: "Mr. Rose, Harwich. Received 8 P.M. and answered immediately by an express which I was just before sending off."

"I have shewn your state to Mr. Arden with your letter and had much conversation with him on the subject; he does not like it by any means, in particular he thinks your own vote doubtful and Mr. Neville's bad; he takes the papers home with him and will write fully on the state and let me have it tomorrow by twelve o'clock, when I will forward it by express. Neither he or I have Carew's book, but I will if possible borrow it and have the extract made which you want. I sent your letters to Mr. Neville and the other gentlemen immediately on receipt. York was carried hollow. Mr. Arden will think of a counsel and send me his name tomorrow with the papers; he could not mention one tonight. The elections in general promise well. Mr. Wilkins however betrayed us most flagrantly.

"I have sent to Lord Howe about the gentleman you alluded to."

1784, March 28—Duke Street, Westminster. George Rose to John Robinson. Endorsed by Robinson "Mr. Rose, Harwich, with Mr. Arden's sentiments. Received 29th 8 A M."

"I send you enclosed the state of the borough of Harwich with Mr. Arden's observations thereon I am most heartily sorry they are not more favorable. I have not been able to get Carew's book, and would not delay sending these papers longer.

"Mr. Arden has not been able yet to hear of a counsel. There. are none in town from the circuit but who are engaged. You may be assured Mr. Bearcroft will not be down, as Mr. Arden has seen him today."

1784, March 29 —Duke Street, Westminster   George Rose to John Robinson   Endorsed by Robinson : " Received 30th 8 P M." " I am rejoiced at your last accounts of Harwich which make me tolerably comfortable on that subject. Mr. Arden still thinks it will be desireable to have a counsel down with you.   He has therefore spoke to Mr. Cowper who will be with you on Wednesday evening or Thursday morning.   He must however have 110 guineas, which is a serious sum.   If Mr. Rigby does not come forward that may be saved.   The business at Seaford has taken a strange turn. General Grant and Andrew John Drummond would not go there, and the people would not elect them in their absence, the consequence of which will be probably that your son-in-law and Sir Peter Parker will be chose, but the election cannot stand, as the proclamation was made on Saturday, and it is to come on tomorrow.   Matters wear a most favorable aspect at present almost everywhere.   Yours in very great haste."

" I cannot find Saunders or Hiblett mentioned in any former letter of yours and consequently do not know where they have votes."

1784, March 30.—Duke Street, Westminster.   George Rose to John Robinson.   Endorsed by Robinson : " Received by express 31, 7 P.M."

" The Ipswich election is taking a perplexing turn   Conwall undertook to reconcile Mr. Middleton to the Corporation and unite him with a friend of theirs.   That has failed, and the gentlemen who act with Mr. Conwall have declared for Mr Cator and Mr Wollaston , the first you know will be a friend, and the latter it is said will.   Mr Middleton, having had however hopes given him, is entitled to support if it will do him good.   You must judge what to do on the spot.   I am sure you will act for the best.   Mr. Middleton is the first object from what has passed.

" At Colchester there is no opposition.   No candidate is yet started against Bullock, who will be an enemy from his connection with your neighbour   We are made easy about your own situation and hope you will have little trouble   You will of course have full accounts from the City of what passed there   Lewis [Lewes] and Watson are safe.   Newnham it is supposed will succeed, and the push will be between Sawbridge and Atkinson.   I have my fears the last will not prevail.   I think Middlesex will do.   Surry and Berkshire are equally in good train.   Sir John Honeywood will stand for Kent. Darrell is safe at Hedon, though he had no assistance from Chaytor. In short, all matters promise better than we hoped."

1784, March 31.—Duke Street, Westminster. George Rose to John Robinson. Endorsed by Robinson : " Received by express 1st April, 6 P.M." " Your letter came in time today to stop Mr. Cowper going down. I am delighted you have cleared your difficulties so well Mr. Nevill and Sir Peter Parker are chosen at Seaford by a majority of one Marlow is safe. Mr Clayton and Sir Thomas Rich had a clear election. Southampton is quite safe ; the opposition is dropped. Windsor is over after an attempt at a brisk opposition from Lord Penryn.

" I explained the Ipswich business to you last night as fully as I could. Nothing can be done to militate against Mr. Middleton as long as there is a possibility of doing him good.

" Measures were taken for Winchelsea, but defeated by the people there deserting their own cause."

1784, April 1, Thursday 45 min past 10.—Duke Street, Westminster George Rose to John Robinson. Endorsed by Robinson : " Received 2nd April, 1784, 4 A M." " You may be assured I have never thought your letters troublesome. This business of Ipswich is a perplexing one Mr Middleton had encouragement given him at a time when he thought the corporation would have been reconciled to him, which Conwall gave great expectations of. If he has no chance it is a pity that Wollaston should be irritated and made an enemy ; at the same time faith must be kept with Middleton. I depend upon your prudence and discretion to manage that and to act as you shall judge proper. Mr. Pitt is gone to Cambridge. I wrote to Mr Cator and you last night , he knew how matters were circumstanced as to Mr Middleton before he went away

" Queenborough is over and as it should be Other accounts this morning promise well. If Sir Robert Smyth is bent on Colchester he will perhaps try the county. Our friends reserve themselves to see what will be done at the meeting on Saturday, where an attendance may be useful.

" I think I told you Marlow ended favorably for Clayton and Sir Thomas Rich. Seaford you know for your son-in-law and Sir Peter Parker. I have lately written so much that I do not remember what I have written to any one."

P.S. " Sam Smith has dropped the City and is gone to Worcester against Rous."

1784, April 2 —— —— George Rose to John Robinson   " You will see by the enclosed how the elections are gone so far.   In addition to them Booth Grey and Ashby are driven from Leicester. Is it not possible to carry Middleton and Cator both for Ipswich ? It is doubtful whether Mr. Woolaston [Wollaston ?] would be a friend."

1784, April 3.—Duke Street, Westminster.   George Rose to John Robinson.   " I rejoice most heartily at your quiet election. Colchester is a strange business ; if Mr Rigby really supported Potter he has summed up all completely.   I hear Middleton and Cator are successful at Ipswich.   If it is true, much must have been owing to you.   I send you a continuation of the returns.   Consider these : Sam Smith and Ward are chosen at Worcester   Two friends are sure at Leicester instead of the old members.   ,

" Mr. Pitt was secure at Cambridge today at 2 o'clock and sanguine hopes of Lord Euston."

P.S.   " Hood 21815—Wray 1975—Fox 1923." [1]

———   ——

The following memoranda are endorsed on the back : " Scarborough, 1784, List of voters—44, of which 8 disqualified placemen ; I vacant ;   I insane, supposed not fit to vote ; I absent abroad ; 33 to poll ; total 44.   If one of them is made comptroller at Whitby there will be only 32 to poll."   The document dates at some time between the dissolution of parliament in 1784 and April 3 of that year, the date of the Scarborough election.

SCARBOROUGH 1784.

-   "Thomas Haggitt, Esquire, Bailiff ; Timothy Otbie, Bailiff and Collector at Scarborough ; John Haley and John Garnet, Coroners ; Thomas Mailing ; John Travis ; James Goland , Thomas Hinderwell, senior ; Joseph Huntress ; James Tindal ; Thomas Hinderwell, junior ;   Ralph Parkin ;   John Robinson, comptroller at Scarborough ; Richard Moorsom, Patent Officer for Hull , Christopher Wilson ; William Williamson, Collector at Bridlington ;

[1] Obviously an error ; see *infra*, p. 123 n.   The vote for Hood at the close of the poll, April 3, was 2185 ; the votes of Fox and Wray are correct.

William Hall, Jerry Wilkinson, junior, John Woodall, and Thomas Stockdale, chamberlains; Thomas Coulson (dead), Comptroller at Whitby; John Harrison, supervisor of Riding officers, William Clarkson; William Duesbury, officer of customs; Leonard Abbot, out of his mind, Valkine Fowler, Richard Sollet; William Parkin; John Coulson, John Sleightholme, custom officer at Whitby, Richard Fox; Thomas Vickerman, Riding officer at Marsk; Henry Travis; Jerry Wilkinson, senior; Thomas Foster; John Parkin; Benjamin Fowler; John Mailing, Anthony Beswick; William Sutton; George Moorsom; Sedgfield Dale, James Cooper; George Hopper.

STATE OF INTEREST AT SCARBOROUGH.

"Number to poll, 34. Lord Tyrconnel and Captain Phipps the present members; Mr. Osbaldstone and Sir Hugh Palliser, declared candidates Lord Tyrconnel will certainly be rechose Captain Phipps was first elected on the relinquishment of Sir Hugh Palliser at the time of his persecution (*sic*), who used his influence among the voters in Captain Phipps's favor. It is (*sic*) now appears that Captain Phipps has but little interest in the borough and has but small chance of succeeding against Mr. Osbaldstone. Mr. Osbaldstone is in the interest of Lord Fitzwilliam and by beginning the canvis (*sic*) very early procured some promises from those who are not friendly to Captain Phipps, and those also who did not know of Sir Hugh Palliser's intending to offer himself

"Sir Hugh Palliser in his canvass appeared to have the good opinion and esteem of the town and corporation, and if he had declared himself sooner he would have been as secure as Lord Tyrconnel; but even now he is supposed to be equal to Mr. Osbaldstone, and it is very probable with a little support will succeed against Mr. Osbaldstone. But if Captain Phipps stands, Mr. Osbaldstone will undoubtedly come in

"It happens that the comptroller's place at Whitby is vacant, which has usually been given to one of Scarborough voters. It is said this place has been applied for by two of the Scarborough voters; if given to either of them, they lose their votes, but if to one of them it will secure two other votes, but if to the other it is not known if it will secure another vote. And yet it is said that if this place is disposed of by Captain Phipps he will still remain very weak. It therefore seems highly necessary that a very exact and impartial inquiry should be made into the present state of Scarborough to see what is best to be done to defeat Mr Osbalidstone. Perhaps *continuing* to keep the office of Comptroller of Whitby open *may* be a prudent measure. The Navy Board used to have influence at Scarborough."

1784, April 7 —Duke Street, Westminster   George Rose to John Robinson. " I send you now the remainder of the returns already received which are not unfavourable as you will see. I cannot compare them with our canvass as you kept it and I have no copy, but I am sure they will turn out much better than our calculation. If you have that canvass with you I wish much you would send it up that we may compare the actual returns with our conjectures. Sturt has declined Dorsetshire and you know Chaytor has done the same in Surry. Berkshire is our own , Sir John Wodehouse starts for Norfolk, and I think we shall have ten good men for Kent Middlesex is almost sure ; if either of our friends is in danger it is Wilkes. Ipswich is wonderfully well settled for which much is due to you. It is monstrously unlucky that Atkinson should lose his election by seven only. I trust however he may yet succeed as I am told near a hundred bad votes are polled, more than half of which are probably against him. Mr Rigby's manœuvre at Colchester was indeed an extraordinary one. You will see by the enclosed from your friend Bamber what is going forward at Liverpool and in Lancashire I trust his son is safe in the former and that his nephew will [be] in the latter. Every possible exertion is making for both Mr. Hughson will not be obstinate I am persuaded when he is spoke to again, which I will do in a few days.

" The Chancellor is a great deal better, well enough to go about I consider the Westminster election now perfectly safe. The state of the poll is Hood 4458, Wray 4117, and Fox 1827.[1] Dover was carried by our friends two to one "

1784, April 8 —Duke Street, Westminster George Rose to

---

[1] Rose's information concerning the progress of the canvass in Westminster seems to have been extremely inaccurate. The state of the poll was published daily in the press *The Morning Chronicle* of May 21, 1784, carried a tabulated list of the votes cast each of the forty days of the poll. At the end of the canvass the vote stood : Hood, 6694 ; Fox, 6234 ; Wray, 5988. At the close of the poll Saturday, April 6, the date of the information supposed to be contained in the above letter, the figures were : Hood, 3936 , Fox, 3413 Wray, 3622

John Robinson. " More good news, York City and County are great events. Penryn is a contra for which I am heartily sorry, but it is impossible to expect to succeed everywhere. I have great fears for Masterman, who now thinks himself in much danger at Bodmyn. Berkshire is *decided* for Pye and Vansittart. All other matters still promise remarkably well."

P.S. " I am persuaded Atkinson has a very flattering prospect of success in his scrutiny." [1]

The following paper, obviously dating about the time of the dissolution of parliament, March 25, 1784, is decribed on its back as : " State of the Number of Vacancies expected and of the Number of Candidates to supply them."

Seats to be Vacated.

74 as per number 1, which are canvassed pro or hopeful, but where the persons having the interest are to bring in the members themselves. Out of this list it is supposed that about 10 seats (as per list) will be left to Mr Pitt's recommendation, either without money or at reasonable rates. These are supposed to be filled by Mr. Pitt's particular friends : 59 seats, as per Number 2, to be purchased, 3 to be deducted for Mr. Elliot, Mr. Walsh, and Mr. Brett, as explained in number 2 ; 56 left, which is the number remaining to be provided for.

Towards this number is to be reckoned those friends now in parliament who may probably chuse to come in upon purchase and which at present appears as follows, exclusive of those who will come in again for seats not here in contemplation : Charles Jenkinson ; George Johnstone ; John Macpherson ; John Pardoe ; Abel Smith ; Henry Beaufoy ; Pepper Arden ; R Jackson , General Luttrell ; The Speaker ; John Purling ; Captain Phipps ; Sir R. Worsley ; Sir John Jarvis ; Sir John Coghill ; Lord Fielding ; John Stevenson ; John Dawes ; Francis Hale ; B. Gascoyne, senior , Lord Mulgrave ; Sir H. Paliser ; Richard Barwell ; Lord Hyde ; Sir F. Sykes , John Fuller ; Lloyd Kenyon ; William Strahan ; Adam Drummond ; John Sinclair ; total 30.

It must be observed that many of these *thirty* would come in

---

[1] Richard Atkinson, who had been beaten by a close vote in London by Alderman Sawbridge, had demanded a scrutiny

for seats reckoned upon as part of the 56, independent of government, but as they may probably all be brought to come in as in friendship to government, the whole number is reckoned upon, as well seats as candidates

30 candidates for 56 seats, leaves 26 seats for new members that will purchase, and the candidates for them to the amount of about 18 appear, not liable to any material objection.   It is therefore supposed that there may probably be found purchasers for nearly the whole number of vacancies, or that the deficiency may not exceed the number of disappointments that may happen in the 59 seats considered as to be had.

So many of the present members as are included in the list of 30 above and do not chuse to purchase will be an addition to the number of vacant seats to be provided for by new candidates to be looked for

N B.   In what precedes there are 3 seats under the influence of Lord Falmouth left out, which are also to be provided for   2 Tregony, 1 Mitchell

---

The following memoranda are endorsed on the back : " Vacancies and candidates to supply them."

Number 1.   Left to themselves   Sir J[ames] Lowther 9 ; Earl Temple 3 ; Earl of Shelburne 3 ; Lord Weymouth 3 ; Duke of Bridgewater 2 ; Lord Sydney 1 ; Lord Gower 3 ; Lord Cornwallis 2 ; The Yorkes 3 , Duke of Rutland 2 ; T[homas] Pitt 2 ; Lord Abingdon 2 ; Lord Pembroke 2 ; Duke of Newcastle 7 ; Lord Falmouth (and Quere 2 Truro) 3 ; Lord Orford 4 , Duke of Northumberland 7 , Mr. Howard 1 ; Lord Sandwich 3 ; Lord Hertford 1 [?] ; Lord Sackville 2 ; Sir John Honeywood 2 ; Lord Aylesbury 4 ; Duke of Chandois 1 ; Hythe 2 ; Total 74 [1]

SEATS TO BE VACATED.

74, as per Number 1, where the persons having the interest will bring in their own members except about 10 reserved for Mr. Pitt's friends.

[1] This total is inaccurate   It should be 75, omitting entirely the seats of Lord Hertford, or 76 if one seat is included for him, or 78, if three seats are counted for him.   The transcript indicates that on the original a "1" is superimposed on a " 3," with two lines drawn horizontally through the entire figure.

59 as per Number —, from which deduct 3, Elliot, Walsh, and Brett, leaving 56.

30 now in, 26 wanted. [Here follows the identical list of names given above, p. 124, with the addition of P. W. Baker]

Appended to the above is another sheet on which is listed what are apparently the names of probable purchasers of the remainder of the fifty-nine seats not provided for. These names are grouped after the name of the person who suggested them.

J[ohn] R[obinson]: Governor Hastings; A. J. Drummond; R. Dent; Barwell, 2 seats; total 4.[1].

Mr. Rose: John Stanley; Kender Mason; Mr. Darrell; Mr. Hunter; total 5.

Mr. A[tkinson]: Himself; P. Metcalfe; Sir S. Hannay; F. Baring; Colonel Balfour; Mr. Ross; Mr. Mackenzie; Mr. Jackson, Admiralty; total 8.

Mr Dundas: Charles Stuart.

Mr. Macpherson: A gentleman whom he can answer for.

R[ichard] A[tkinson]: Wraxall; Major Osborne; W. Smith; Langston; Fraser.

J[ohn] R[obinson]: Cator; Jere. Crutchley; Major Deveil; Mr. Way, 1,500l.; Boehm; Boehm, 1,500l.; Mr. Rodney, Mr. Steele.[2]

This is a single sheet endorsed in pencil: "Candidates." Contrast the above list from which it differs only in some matters of detail and in some omissions.

Mr. Robinson: Governor Hastings; Andrew John Drummond; R. Dent; Captain Barwell; total 4.

---

[1] Apparently Barwell, one of the influential East India directors, agreed to bring in one member in addition to the one mentioned in list given above.

[2] The second lists by Atkinson and Robinson are in a different column on the same page. Apparently Way was willing to spend as much as 1,500l., and Boehm was willing to purchase one seat and another to the amount of 1,500l.

Mr. Rose: John Hanley, Kender Mason, Mr. Darrell; Mr. Hunter; total 5.[1]

Mr. Atkinson: Himself, if not otherwise provided for; P. Metcalfe; Sir S. Hannay; Francis Baring; Colonel Balfour; Mr. Ross; Mr. Mackenzie; Mr. Jackson, Admiralty; total 8

Mr. Dundas: Charles Stuart.

Mr. Macpherson: A gentleman whom he says he can be answerable for, but, Quere.

The following is on a separate sheet endorsed: "Memorandums for Mr Robinson."

Wallingford . .	To learn whether Sir F. Sykes will stand.
Aylesbury . . .	Bacon ditto.
Helston . . .	Barwell ditto.
Poole	To write to Lister.
Malden	Mr. Strutt. N B. The scheme about Mr. Hamilton will not do.
Northampton . .	H. Drummond about Lord Compton and opposing Lord Lucan.
Stockbridge . .	Mr Robinson to see two friends.

The following memoranda endorsed on the back: "Extracts of seats that come easy and Names classed," is manifestly a product of the canvass incident to the parliamentary election of 1784.

EXTRACTS FROM THE LISTS.

Persons supposed to be brought in at little expence: Mr. Jenkinson; Mr. Kenyon; Mr. Arden; The Speaker; Mr. Gascoyne, senior; Captain Phipps

Places that cost little but the expences of the election: Saltash, present members, C. Jenkinson and Sir Grey Cooper; Queenborough, present members, Sir C. Frederick and Sir W. Rawlinson; Dartmouth, present members, Mr. Holdsworth and Mr. Brett; Harwick; Plymouth; Pontefract; Scarborough.

Persons who will pay 1,500l. or perhaps somewhat more, or,

---

[1] The total number of Rose's list in this as in the above paper is stated inaccurately unless one of the men named had agreed to purchase two seats, of which there is no indication.

having paid largely last time, it may be right to let in as easy as may be : A. J. Drummond , Mr. Boehm ; Mr. Way ; G. Rodney ; G. Jackson ; T. Somers Cocks ; A. Drummond ; J. Stevenson ; J. Dawes ; Mr. Beaufoy ; J. Macpherson ; J. Pardoe ; Abel Smith ; Sir Francis Sykes ; J. Fuller ; Mr. Steele's friends ; Mr Charles Stuart and Mr. Colt, Mr. Dundas' friends ; Mr. Wraxall ; General Grant ; Lord Parker.

Persons that will pay 2,000 or 2,500 or perhaps 3,000*l* : Governor Hastings ; (Query, also Major Scott) ; Mr. Barwell ; Mr. Barwell , J. Cator , J. Crutchley ; Major D'veil ; Mr. R. Boehm ; Mr. J. Stanley , Mr. Kinder Mason , Mr. Darrell ; Mr. Hunter ; R Atkinson ; P. Metcalfe ; Sir S. Hannay ; F. Baring ; Colonel Balfour ; H. Ross ; Major Osborne ; William Smith ; Mr. Langstone ; S. Fraser ; R. Dent and Mr. Mackenzie, Mr. Macpherson's friends (Query, yet).

The following memoranda, endorsed on the back : " Last State of Seats and candidates," and therefore probably dating some time in April, 1784, begins with a list which includes at least a part of the boroughs that made up list number 2, mentioned above, but which list is not found in the transcripts.

Seats reckoned certain for money : Saltash 2 ; Queensborough 2 ; Liskeard 2 ; St. Germans 1 ; Grampound 2 ; Luggershall 1 ; Dartmouth 1 ; Harwich 1 ; Plymouth 1 ; Pontefract 1 ; Lostwithiel 2 , Bossiney 1 ; Fowey 1 ; Plympton 2, [the " 2 " is drawn through with a pencil and " 1 " placed after it] ; West Loo 2 ; Camelford 2 ; St. Ives 1 ; Minehead 1 ; Newton 1 ; Lymington 1 ; Malmesbury 2 ; Hastings 2 ; Rye 2 ; Seaford 2 ; Sandwich 1 ; Romney 1 , total 38. Chances : Wareham 2 , Thirsk 1 , Horsham 1 ; total 42.

Friends already in for some of these seats : C. Jenkinson ; James Macpherson, *Camelford* ; John Pardoe ; Abel Smith ; H. Beaufoy ; P. Arden ; R. Jackson, *Romney* ; Sir R. Worsley, *Newton* ; P. Stephens, *Sandwich* ; T. Somers Cocks ; 10 old members for these seats.

Other old members who will probably pay if they do not get in again for their present seats : Speaker for Winchelsea ; John Stevenson and John Dawes, Tregony , B. Gasgoyne, senior, Truro ;

Captain Phipps, Scarborough, Sir F. Sykes, Shaftesbury; John Fuller, Southampton; Lloyd Kenyon, Hindon; A. Drummond, Aberbrothock; J. Sinclair, Caithness; I. Boyd, G Rodney

NEW CANDIDATES

J[ohn] R[obinson]: Governor Hastings, *West Looe*; A J. Drummond, *Query*, Barwell, *Query*; Barwell, *Wendover*; *Bensley*; J. Cator and Jere. Crutchley, *Stockbridge*; Major Macbeach; Mr. Boehm, Mr. Boehm, 1,500*l* ; Mr. Way, 1,500*l* ; total 10.

G[eorge] R[ose] · John Stanley, Kender Mason [1], Mr. Darrell, *Query*; Mr Hunter, *Query*, total 4.

T[homas] Steele : 1

Mr. Dundas   Charles Stuart [1], General Grant; Mr Colt [1]; total 3.

R[ichard] A[tkinson] · R Atkinson, P. Metcalfe; Sir S Hannay; F Baring; Colonel Balfour, Hercules Ross; N. W. Wraxall; Major Osborne; William Smith, *Sudbury*; Mr. Langston, Simon Fraser, *Minehead*; total 11

James Macpherson : 1. Total certain : 30

Probable : R. Dent, G. Rodney [1]; G. Jackson, *Rochester*, Mr Mackenzie; total 4.

William Peter Baker, Penn Curzon, *Leominster*; Mr. Turner.[2]

1784, October 1 —Duke Street, Westminster. George Rose to John Robinson. "There cannot be the smallest doubt of its being a desirable object to secure the place, and I really think it will be worth while for the two gentlemen to come up Considering what Harbin has done it is perhaps right he should be with them I think it is perfectly fair to have two if possible as the present one has no pretence to favor. That is however a subject to consider a little of. In the meantime pray encourage the parties as much as possible to keep in the right way, they have infinitely more inducements to it than to go where they threaten.

"There would be no great difficulty in keeping the cutter for one of their friends as Mr. Harbin desires, but that she ceases to be in

---

[1] The names of Mason, Stuart, Colt, and Rodney are drawn through in ink

[2] The last three names are accredited to nobody. The italicized names of boroughs in this list appear in the transcript in pencil and are apparently so in the original. The "Query" is also in pencil where italicized.

government service and is now on contract. We have therefore you know nothing to do with the commander or officers of her."

P.S. "I did not get your letter last night till some time too late for the post, or I would have answered it then."

1785, October 3.—Great George Street. George Rose to John Robinson "I trust you will have the goodness to forgive me for troubling you again on the subject of the book containing the whole patronage of the Treasury, which I believe was compiled by Mr. Rowe Mr. Pitt is beyond measure anxious to have it and will be very much obliged to you for the communication of it. We shall otherwise be compelled to write to all the offices and gather up the intelligence by scraps as we can

"Our friend Beresford and his wife are both here, but are on the wing on Wednesday by the way of Scotland. Orde is also here you know. I really think things are in very good train in Ireland.

"The peace between the Emperor and the Dutch is completed, the latter paying 10,000,000 of Florins for liberty to keep their own town of Maestricht."

1788, October 18 —Great George Street George Rose to John Robinson Endorsed by Robinson : "Received 20th. Answered immediately 210*l* draft." "You have already a circular application on the subject of this letter, I believe, but the importance of it obliges me to trouble you myself on it. The late election for Westminster [1] and the investigation of all the means used for preventing the success of Lord Hood have been and must be attended with so considerable an expence as to compel the necessity of subscription to defray it, and it is of real importance that a considerable sum should be raised for that purpose with as little delay as possible. You will therefore I trust have the goodness to excuse my troubling you on the business which nothing less than such a necessity could induce me to do. I do not mean however by any means to urge you to contribute. I wish only that you should be apprised that the consequences of *this* election are likely to extend very much beyond Westminster, and that the expectation of defeating in future such practices as prevailed at

---

[1] A by-election earlier in 1788 in which Lord John Townshend, standing in the interest of the Whigs, successfully contested the election of Lord Hood, the administration candidate. The two parties compromised the constituency before the general election of 1790, each party agreeing to be contented with one seat.

the *last* must in a great measure depend upon those being detected and exposed, the certainty of which cannot be doubted if the subscription shall enable proper measures being taken.   I trust however in any event you will excuse this freedom, and I beg only to repeat that the benefit arising from the contributions will be very much encreased by their being made early.   The first *private* friend who subscribed gave two hundred pounds, but anything will be thankfully received."

P.S   " Subscriptions are received in the name of Edmund Estcourt, Esquire, at Messrs Drummonds, Charing Cross, and at Crofts, Devaynes and Dawes in Pall Mall "

1784, October 20—Syon Hill   John Robinson to George Rose. Pencil draft of reply to above letter.   " I have this morning been favored with your letter which I loose not an hour *to answer*.   What you mention and more shall not on my part be wanting to prove the sincerety and zeal I have for Mr Pitt's administration and how much I am my Dear sir &c "

Instruction added : " N.B.   *Answer* by sending inclosed a draft to G[eorge] Rose, Esquire, or bearer on Messrs. Drummond for 200 guineas."

1788, October 30 —Great George Street.   George Rose to John Robinson   " You know by experience how painful a thing it is to communicate the impossibility of complying with anxious and earnest applications ; it is not to be described how uncomfortable I feel on such occasions.   With respect to the coast waiters place now vacant there are more than ordinary embarrassments.   Mr. Hawkins' brother has positive promise of *more than three years standing*, and Mr. Grigby nearly as long ; Lord Grey de Wilton two years and a half.   These are all prior to yours, and the former I really believe cannot be put by without positive offence.   When I have the pleasure of seeing you we will consider if some other situation cannot be thought of for your Harwich friend equally desireable.   I need not say that Mr. Pitt will be glad to [make] any such arrangement that is possible

" I am so sure that you will not be less forward to assist us on account of an *involuntary* refusal that I do not hesitate to beg you will intercede with Mr. Stephenson to give his best support to Lord Carysfort in Huntingdonshire for whose success Mr. Pitt has more than ordinary anxiety."

1789, June 23.—Old Palace Yard.   George Rose to John Robin-

son.* " You may be perfectly sure that Mr. Crowder will be re-
appointed to the Lottery   I will take the earliest opportunity I
can of bringing Mr. Jackson to a point about Colchester.

" We are in a sad embarrassment about the coal meter at Maning-
tree.   Bramston has asked it with extreme earnestness for a man
protected in a particular manner by the late Mr Rigby, and Mr.
Pitt has made it a rule always to give out-laying places to the
members for counties, confining the patronage of seaports to the
towns in which the offices are situated, I mean to the Head Port
sending the members.   I have stated your recommendation to
Bramston, but he is still pressing for the office.

" You will hear through other channels that the Westminster
committee go on.   The proposal was the most extraordinary one
that ever was thought of.   I have no doubt but that Mr. Pitt will
approve of directions being immediately given for you to proceed
in the whole of the works stated in your memorial of the 23d of
March, and I will take care that regular authority shall be sent
for that purpose."

1789, December 15.—Cuffnells.   George Rose to John Robinson.
" We have a very sharp contest in this county, and I understand
Mr. John Blackburn of Scotch Yard has a good estate in it.   Pray
have the goodness therefore to apply to him *immediately*, or get
his friend, Mr. John Stephenson, to do so, in favor of Sir William
Heathcote, who is opposed by Lord John Russell, an entire stranger
in Hampshire.   It is very important to have single votes for Sir
William if possible ; as I should have said the struggle is for the
general election when the Baronet will have to contend with Jer-
voise and Lord John."

P S   " I shall be in town in a day or two."

SECRET AND SPECIAL SERVICE
ACCOUNTS

SECTION IV
SECRET AND SPECIAL SERVICE ACCOUNTS

THE papers included in this section have little connection with those in the three preceding sections save the facts that Mr. Stevens transcribed them from the papers left by John Robinson and that much of the money itemized in these accounts was expended in the management of parliamentary elections. The correspondence relating to the payment of the debts of Lord North is included in this section because this payment was a special expenditure from the private funds of the king, and it would seem to belong here rather than among the papers relating more directly to parliamentary business

The following five papers relate primarily to the expenditure of George III and his predecessor for secret and special services The first paper is descriptive of those that follow and is apparently the work of Robinson That and the second, third, and fifth papers appear to have been copied in full ; it is so pencilled on the transcript of the first. An abstract only was taken of the fourth, and there is no evidence of any transcription whatever from the remaining documents Most of this information was probably collected for use in the debate incident to the payment of the debt on the Civil List in 1777, and much of it was printed in parliamentary papers at that time.

I

Treasury papers and accounts which may be of very essential use to a man of business to at times look into for useful information.[1]

---

[1] Robinson probably prepared this table of contents of a packet of excerpts from treasury records at a date later than when they were compiled, perhaps after he was out of office This prefatory memorandum is understandable under those circumstances.

1752, October to October, 1768: Account of Money issued for Secret and Special Service.

1751, January 1 to 5 January, 1777: Account showing the extra Revenues Etc.

1762, April 5 to 5 July, 1766: Account of the Debt on the Civil List.

1769, January 5 to January 5, 1777: Account of Monies issued for Secret and Special Services.

An account of Money paid for His Majesty's Service and for Bills of Exchange by Mr. Davis et al, in three years to 5 January, 1760, and in 12 years to 5 January, 1773.

1772, January 9: A State of the Expence of the Foreign Ministers, exclusive of extra extraordinaires.

1761–1776: Account of the charge incurred for Foreign Ministers for sixteen years from 1760

II

Account of all Monies which have been issued for Secret and Special Service from October, 1752, to October, 1768.

	Secretaries of State			Secretaries of the Treasury			Divers persons			Totals.		
	l	*s*	*d*	*l.*	*s.*	*d.*	*l.*	*s*	*d*	*l*	*s.*	*d.*
From October, 1752, to October, 1753	6,000			48,890						55,890		
1754	5,891	13	4	70,300						76,191	13	4
1755	6,000			78,770						84,770		
1756	6,073	8		126,315	11	6				132,388	19	6
1757	7,282	14	9¾	66,000			31,717	5	6	105,000		3¾
1758	6,000			58,540			36,242	11		100,782	11	
1759	6,000			69,360			1,487	17	8¾	76,847	17	8¾
1760	6,000			73,880	14					79,880	14	
Total	49,247	16	1¾	593,056	5	6	69,447	14	2¾	711,751	15	10½
Medium of 8 years	6,155	19	6	74,132	0	8¼	8.680	19	3¼	88,968	19	5¾
Add the annual sum of which was issued by the receipt of the Post Office revenue to the Secretary of the Post Office for his Majesty's Service										4,510		
										93,478	19	5¾

There was issued in the Name of John Nicholl, Esquire, (who is here included under the article of *Divers Persons*) during the above 8 years the sum of 28,408 10 6, the average of which for 8 years is 3,551 1 3¾. If this is added to the money issued to the Secretary to the Treasury it will amount to 77,683 2.

	Secretaries of State and of Post Office.			Secretaries to the Treasury.			Divers persons.			Total		
	l.	*s.*	*d.*	*l.*	*s.*	*d.*	*l.*	*s.*	*d.*	*l*	*s.*	*d*
Issue to the Post Office commenced this year,												
1761 .	8,639	10	6	57,735	14	6	10,507	17	6	76,883	2	6
1762 .	13,218	9	10	48,000			42,188	19	6	103,407	9	4
1763 .	10,973	18	11¼	65,420			15,000			91,393	18	11¼
1764 .	10,706	11	5¼				57,905	0	6	68,611	11	11¼
1765	13,960	19	1	16,425	12		21,005	10	6	51,392	1	7
1766	8,991	7	1	36,216	16	6	16,571	5		61,779	8	7
1767	12,920	7	11	29,633	5		3,721	14	5	46,275	7	4
1768	14,599	18	1	46,860			8,203	1	8	69,662	19	9
Total .	94,011	2	11	300,291	8		175,103	9	1	569,406		
Medium of 8 years . .	11,751	7	9	37,536	8	6	21,887	18	7½	71,175	15	

There was issued in the name of John Nicholl (who is here included under the article of *Divers Persons*), during the above period of 8 years the sum of 66,836 10, the average of which for 8 years is 8,354 11 3. If this is added to the money issued to the Secretaries to the Treasury it will amount to 45,890 19 9.

III

An accompt showing the extra revenues applied for his late Majesty's service in 8 years between the first of January, 1751, and the first of January, 1759, and the extra revenues applied for his present Majesty's use, as well for secret service as other purposes, for 8 years from the 1st of January, 1761, to the 1st of January, 1769, and from the 5th of January, 1769, to 5th of January, 1777, with a médium taken upon each 8 years of expence and a comparison of the same.

In 8 Years to 1st January, 1759

	l.	*s*	*d.*
Out of 4½ per cent.	103,109	19	9¾
Rent of Savoy Hospital	260	6	6¼
Rent of Lands given to superstitious uses . .	1,074	16	2
Duchy of Cornwall	40,000		
Virginia Quit Rents	30,223	10	
Revenue of Gibraltar	7,000		
	181,668	12	6
Medium for those 8 years	22,708	11	6

In 8 Years to 1st January, 1769

	l.	s.	d.
Out of 4½ per cent.	90,699	6	6
Dutchy of Cornwall	66,978	11	2
Revenue of Gibraltar	33,720	19	6
Virginia Quit Rents	28,200		
Money from Guadeloupe	12,481	4	
Casual Revenues in Barbadoes	2,000		
Late King's arrears	172,605	5	4½
	406,685	6	6½
Medium for those 8 years	50,835	13	3

In 8 Years to 5th January, 1777

	l.	s.	d
Out of 4½ per cent.	60,045	6	
Revenues of the late King	1,149	6	1
Revenue of the Dutchy of Cornwall	95,450		
Virginia Quit Rents	45,358	2	
Revenue of Gibraltar	5,076	11	4¾
Money received from Guadaloupe	183	13	½
Casual Revenues of Barbadoes	1,000		
Nova Scotia Quit Rents	430		
Georgia Quit Rents	160		
Sale of Lands in Georgia	570		
	209,422	18	6¼
Medium for those 8 years	26,177	17	3

	l.	s.	d.
The medium of the 8 years to the 1st January, 1769	50,835	13	3
Ditto of the 8 years (of the late King) to 1st January, 1759	22,708	11	6
More applied in the first 8 years of his present Majesty	28,127	1	9
The medium of the 8 years to the 1st January, 1769	50,835	13	3
Ditto of the 8 years to the 5th January, 1777	26,177	17	3
Less applied in the last 8 years	24,657	16	

IV

The paper of which the following indicates merely the totals is endorsed : " An account of the Debt on the Civil List as it stood on the 5th day of April, 1762, the 5th day of April, 1763, the 5th day of July, 1765, and the 5th day of July, 1766, together with an account of the arrears of his late Majesty's Civil List revenues unapplied and his present Majesty's Civil List cash remaining in the Exchequer at those several times." There is on the abstract this note, apparently by Mr. Stevens: ." The bulk of this debt appears to have been incurred by foreign ministers ; sums paid for secret service come amongst the smaller amounts."

	l.	*s.*	*d.*
Debt on April 5, 1762	172,451	12	2¾
Debt on April 5, 1763	231,089	8	9¾
Debt on July 5, 1765	331,665		8¾
Debt on July 5, 1766 . . .	388,389	5	10

V

The following paper is endorsed : " An Accompt of all Monies issued by any of his Majesty's Receivers or Collectors or their agents for his Majesty's Secret and Special service from the 5th day of January, 1769, to the 5th day of January, 1777."

In the year ended the 5th day of January,
1770, To Thomas Bradshaw, Esquire, for his Majesty's Special Service . . . .
1771, To ditto   for ditto. . . . .
1772, To John Robinson, Esquire, for ditto . . . .
1773, To ditto   for ditto . . . .
1773, To Osgood Hanbury, Esquire, for ditto . . . .
1774, To John Robinson, Esquire, for ditto . . . .
1774, To Osgood Hanbury, Esquire, for ditto . . . .
1775, To John Robinson, Esquire, for ditto . . . .
1775, To John Robinson, Esquire, for his Majesty's Secret Service . . . .
1775, To Osgood Hanbury, Esquire, for his Majesty's Special Service . . . . . .
1776, To Osgood Hanbury, Esquire, for ditto . . . .
1776, To Grey Cooper, Esquire, for ditto . . . .
1776, To John Robinson, Esquire, for ditto . . . .
1777, To John Robinson, Esquire, for ditto . . . .

To this endorsement is added, apparently at a subsequent time : This paper not now material to be looked into, being included in and ated in paper Number 1. Presented to Parliament "

Sums issued by the Receiver of

Revenue of the Duchy of Cornwall	Virginia Quit Rents	Nova Scotia Quit Rents	Georgia Quit Rents	Revenue of Gibraltar.	Casual Revenues of Barbadoes.	Money arising by sale of Lands in Georgia.	Totals.
l s d	l s d	l s d	l s d	l s. d	$l.$ s d	$l.$ s d	l s d
,000	4,240	.	.	.	. .	. .	15,240
,000	1,048	. .	. .	. .	. .		18,048
,700	10,000	.	. .	.	. .	.	18,700
,000	5,900	150		958 7 4¼	. .	)	
. .	900	. .		. .	. .	)	20,908 7 4¼
,800	8,444	.	.	. .	1,000	570)	
. .	486		.		. .	}	23,300
,000	6,528 12	. .	. .	. .	. .	. .)	
. .	.	. .	160		.	}	15,080 2
. .	391 10		.	.	.	.)	
.	420	.	.			)	
,000	4,000	. .	. .		. .	. }	19,700
. .	3,000	280	.	-	. .	. .)	
,950		. .	.		. .		12,950
,450	45,358 2	430	160	958 7 4¼	1,000	570	143,926 9 4¼

The following undated statement was probably prepared incidental to the debate on the payment of the debts on the Civil List in 1777. It is endorsed : " Secret Service by Secretaries of the Treasury and by Secretaries of State from 5 November, 1688, to Lady day, 1702 " The first column indicates the years in which the sums were issued, the second the total amount issued in that year to the " Secretaries of the Treasury," the third the sums issued to " Particular Persons by his Majesty's Warrant under his Royal sign manual," the fourth the total of these two columns, and the fifth the sums issued to " secretaries of State " These last items are not added in the totals and appear in a separate place on the original sheet.

From November 5, 1688,					
to Michaelmas,	1689	. . .	88,238	20,000	108,238	4,000
	1690	. . .	113,049		113,049	2,000
	1691 .		65,414		65,414	6,503
	1692	. .	28,101	12,000	40,101	4,500
	1693		56,959		56,959	4,050
	1694	.	37,106		37,106	6,500
	1695 .		16,770		16,770	6,660
	1696	.	21,733		21,733	13,500
	1697 . .		25,383	12,300	37,683	7,000
	1698		27,412		27,412	2,000
	1699		38,083	12,300	40,383	7,000
	1700		39,541	6,000	45,541	5,750
	1701		39,668	11,100	50,768	5,000
To Lady Day	1702		28,860	84,000	112,860	2,500
			616,317	157,700	774,017	76,963

The following letters, which are in a separate packet, are endorsed : " June and July   Some papers on a secret service with Lord North, Mr. Wedderburn, the Attorney General, Mr. Pulteney, and Mr. Whateley, transacted by me by Lord North's special orders, purpose most secret and confidential, all settled by Lord North's orders." The initials of Robinson are affixed to this endorsement Mr. Stevens thought that these letters pertain to the transactions incidental to the payment of Lord North's debts by the king, an opinion which is probably correct.

Of the sixteen papers which this packet apparently contains, all written and signed personally by the men whose names are affixed, Mr. Stevens transcribed only seven ; he merely quotes Robinson's endorsement on the back of the rest.   Since Robinson's endorsements are an indication of the contents of the documents that were not transcribed, they are given in proper chronological order with the letters that were copied.

1778, March 24.—Henry Drummond to [John Robinson].   Endorsed · " 24th March, 1778.   Messrs. Drummond with notes for 20,000*l* for my draft of this day on them payable to bearer, which notes I instantly sent away to Mr. Wedderburne on the trust vested in him and in Mr. Pulteney by Lord North's order "

1778, March 24.—Alexander Wedderburn to [John Robinson] Endorsed : " 24th March, 1778.   Mr. Wedderburne, acknowledging the notes coming safe."

1778, June 12 —Alexander Wedderburn to John Robinson. Endorsed : " 12 June, Mr. Attorney General.   Answered 13th ditto."   " I spoke to Mr. Pulteney about the business you mentioned to me some time, which I thought had been finished and that he had put the receipt into your hands.   He talked to me about a sum that was to be paid for some purpose which I did not wish to have explained.   But I should be very glad to have the whole business finished as soon as it can."

1778, June 25.—Alexander Wedderburn to John Robinson. Endorsed : " 25th June, 1778.   Mr. Attorney General.   Money and Cert., a sum.   Received 26th and answered same day."   " I wrote to you about ten days ago to beg that I might be discharged of my trust in the money paid to Mr. Whately's and invested in the subscription   I mentioned to you then that I had spoken to Mr. Pulteney about it, who was desirous of concurring with me, but at the same time talked to me about a sum of 300*l*. which Lord North had agreed to pay on some account, and I wished therefore that you would be so good as to settle that matter and receive from Mr. Pulteney the banker's receipt, which is in his hands.

" It will be rather awkward for me to apply to Mr. Pulteney, that matter unsettled, and I have no doubt he will bring the receipt to you the moment he hears from you, after which, if it is necessary for me to sign any order or indorse the certificates, I will go any morning to Lombard Street, for I do assure you it will be a great satisfaction to me to erase this and every other trace of the affairs of the last six months from my mind."

1778, June 27.—William Pulteney to John Robinson. Endorsed : " Mr Pulteney. Received 29th June and answered 30th ditto. Vide copy." " I received your note last night very late and went to the City early this morning in order to know what was necessary to be done for a compleat transference of the scrip. I found that it was necessary that we should sign our names on the back of the receipt, and I therefore brought the banker with me and all the receipts to Lincoln's Inn Fields, where we both signed, and then we returned them to the banker that he might deliver them and the cash not yet paid on account of the scrip to our order ; we have both signed an order accordingly directing the banker to deliver the whole to the bearer, which is in my possession to be given to you whenever you fix an hour for that purpose. I came to your house in order to deliver it, but you had just set out for the country.

" You say in your letter that you *had said* you had received Lord North's orders concerning another matter, but you never said so to me, either in what you formerly wrote to me or in any conversation. The last time I talked to you, which was in the House of Commons the day before the prorogation, you said you had not then mentioned it to Lord North, and I have not seen nor heard from you since, and therefore the delay has hitherto lain at your own door.

" I must set you right in another point. You suppose that the other matter relates to expences. Now I wish you to understand that I neither claim nor will accept of any expences incurred by myself ; the money is for another person, and Lord North knows that to be the case."[1]

1778, June 30.—Syon Hill. John Robinson to William Pulteney. Endorsed : " Copy of my letter to Mr. Pulteney." " The letter you favoured me with was yesterday brought to me hither. I shall be in town tomorrow, and if you will give me leave, I will do myself the pleasure of calling on you tomorrow between 12 and 1 o'clock to settle the business. I was very sensible when I made use of the word *expences* that the sum to be paid was not for *your* expences but what was given by you to another person for certain expences, and therefore I am sorry you should apprehend I meant the word as applicable to you, for it certainly was not. And what I mentioned in my letter to the Attorney General, that I *had said* I had received Lord North's orders Etc., referred not to you either but to what I had said to the Attorney General, to whom, if I am not very much mistaken, I said so on the night of the King's birthday

[1] See pp. 186–7.

This, I hope, will set these two things right to your satisfaction."

1778, July 2.—½ past 2 o'clock. William Pulteney to John Robinson. Endorsed : " Mr. Pulteney's note wrote from my house to me at the treasury on the business of settling the accounts. Received at the treasury 4 p.m. 2d and went to him immediately and settled the account except as to the Omnium, which remains to be settled when sold." " I have got the business done. If you can come in a quarter of an hour I will wait for you, but I have a particular engagement which prevents my staying longer. If you should not come in that time, I shall be at home at 8 o'clock this evening and glad to see you."

1778, July 3 —William Whately to William Pulteney.   Endorsed : " Sale of Omnium."

1778, July 6.—William Whately to William Pulteney   Endorsed : " Sale of Omnium."

1778, July 8.—William Whately to William Pulteney.   Endorsed : " On the sale of Omnium."

1778, July 14 —Bath House.   William Pulteney to John Robinson. Endorsed : " Mr. Pulteney.   Answered and seen."   " Upon my coming to town I found your letter inclosing some papers.   I am sorry I had not the good fortune to be at home when you called. I think Lord North has not returned all the letters I sent him.

" Before I left town I received a letter from Mr. Whately, which I send you, giving an account of the sale of the remainder of the stock, but I could not then go to the City to receive the money I called at his banking shop today in my way from the country and have received the amount which I am impatient to deliver to you.   He could not make out the account at full length whilst I stayed but promised to send it by the penny post, and I suppose I shall have it before I see you, but he gave me the gross sums.

" You will please to fix your hour for receiving the money and remember that I am to have a copy of the account which I gave you with the last payment."

1778, July 17.—London.   William Pulteney to John Robinson. Endorsed : " Mr. Pulteney, with General Account of sales of 20,000l. scrip.   Received 17th in the morning and answered in evening "   This letter contained an enclosure not transcribed but described as : " Broker's account of the sales of the stock   20,000l. Omnium."   " I now send you the broker's account of the sales of the stock sent me yesterday by the bankers, which you can

L

examine with the letters I sent you. The ballance agrees with what they paid me.

"I understand from Mr. Chalmers that Lord North proposes to consider today at the Board what sort of reward Mr. Chalmers [1] should have for the very important services he rendered to the revenue and to the trade of this great kingdom by the improvements made by his advice and assistance in the Post Office. It seems evident to me that Mr. Nelthrop [2] cannot be longer continued in the Scotch commission of the customs without occasioning an outcry, and nobody can be more fit to fill that office than Mr. Chalmers This measure would do credit to administration, as on the other hand there would be a great degree of harshness in leaving any longer unrewarded such services as those of Mr. Chalmers."

1778, July 17.—William Pulteney to John Robinson. "Will be at home from 5 o'clock p.m ; hopes he has made copy of first account."

1778, July 23.—William Pulteney to John Robinson. "Will be at home all the morning and glad to see Mr. Robinson."

1778, July 24 —John Robinson to William Pulteney. "Acknowledgment given to Mr Pulteney on settling the account about the 20,000." [3]

Mr. Stevens made a facsimile of the following account book, which seemed to him to be of greater value than it probably really is, since all the information it contains is accessible in the Treasury papers at the Public Record Office   However, it is given here with a pagination uniform with the original book.   Sheets number thirteen and following, including the first half of number eighteen, are missing, but Mr. Stevens says in a pencilled note on the facsimile and also in his letter to the Marquess of Abergavenny that this is not a defect, the missing pages being blank in the original book. The contents of the part of number eighteen that is reproduced nevertheless indicates that some items that went before are missing. The title page of the facsimile is apparently, in part at least, the work of Mr. Stevens.   It reads

---

[1] Probably George Chalmers, then a pamphleteer, later a government clerk, biographer of Paine, etc.

[2] William Nelthorpe.

[3] The last three items were not transcribed. The quotations given are abstracts by the copyist.

"Account of Money issued for His Majesty's Secret and Special Service between the 5th of January, 1769, and the 30th of March, 1782, and Account of Monies paid, 1775 to 1782, for the Relief and Benefit of sundry American Officers and others who have suffered on Account of their Attachment to His Majesty's Government.

"Abergavenny Manuscripts at Eridge Castle

"*Notes* This small volume, in red morocco, gilt edges, is much stained, and the paper rotten and discoloured by damp."

I

An Accompt of the Money issued for His Majesty's Secret and Special Service to the Persons undermentioned between the 5th of January, 1769, and the 5th of January, 1777.

	Secret Service.			Special Service.			Total		
	l	*s.*	*d*	*l*	*s*	*d.*	*l.*	*s*	*d*
In the year ended 5th January, 1770,									
To Grey Cooper, Esquire . . .	42,000			18,219	12	6			
To Thomas Bradshaw, Esquire	4,000			15,240					
	46,000			33,459	12	6			
				46,000					
							79,459	12	6
In the year ended 5th January, 1771,									
To Grey Cooper, Esquire .	26,000			10,537	2	6			
Thomas Bradshaw, Esquire	8,000			22,261	5				
Milward Rowe, Esquire .	4,000								
	38,000			32.798	7	6			
				38.000					
							70,798	7	6
In the year ended 5th January, 1772,									
To Grey Cooper, Esquire .	20,213	5	6	4,213	5	6			
John Robinson, Esquire .	11,000			26,989	15	8			
	31,213	5	6	31,203	1	2			
				31,213	5	6			
							62,416	6	8
In the year ended 5th January, 1773,									
To Grey Cooper, Esquire	12,000			6,324	1				
John Robinson, Esquire	21,000			20,008	7	4¼			
	33,000			26,332	8	4¼			
				33,000					
							59,332	8	4¼
Borne forward . . .							272,006	15	¼

2

	Secret Service	Special Service	Total
	l. *s.* *d*	*l* *s.* *d.*	*l* *s.* *d.*
Brought forward .	..	..	272,006 15 ¼
In the year ended 5th January, 1774,			
To Grey Cooper, Esquire .	12,000	5,272 16 6	
John Robinson, Esquire .	24.000	22,814	
	36,000	28,086 16 6	
		36,000	
			64,086 16 6
In the year ended 5th January, 1775,			
To Grey Cooper, Esquire . . .	23,000		
John Robinson, Esquire . .	25,160	20,722 11 8½	
	48,160	20,722 11 8½	
		48,160	
			68,882 11 8½
In the year ended 5th January, 1776,			
To Sir Grey Cooper, Baronet .	19,000	16,000	
John Robinson, Esquire . .	11,000	3,280	
	30,000	19,280	
		30,000	
			49,280
In the year ended 5th January, 1777,			
To Sir Grey Cooper, Baronet .	21,000		
John Robinson, Esquire .	22,000	12,950	
	43,000	12,950	
		43,000	
			55,950
			510,206 3 2¾

3

AN ACCOMPT OF THE MONEY ISSUED FOR HIS MAJESTY'S SECRET
AND SPECIAL SERVICE TO THE PERSONS UNDERMENTIONED
BETWEEN THE 5TH OF JANUARY, 1777, AND THE 5TH OF JANUARY
[30TH OF MARCH, 1782].

	Secret Service.			Special Service			Total		
	l.	*s.*	*d*	*l*	*s*	*d.*	*l*	*s*	*d*
In the year ended 5th January, 1778,									
To Sir Grey Cooper, Baronet .	22,000								
To John Robinson, Esquire	35,000			13,494		8½			
				57,000					
							70,494		8½
In the year ended 5th January, 1779,									
To Sir Grey Cooper. . . .	23,000								
To John Robinson, Esquire .	28,000			35,964					
				51,000					
							86,964		
In the year ended 5th January, 1780,									
To Sir Grey Cooper. .	16,000								
To John Robinson, Esquire .	46,000			18,640					
				62,000					
							80,640		
							238,098		8½
In the year ended 5th January, 1781,									
To Sir Grey Cooper. . .	22,000								
To John Robinson, Esquire .	15,000			11,000					
				37,000					
							48,503		
In the year ended 5th January, 1782,									
To Sir Grey Cooper. . .	15,000								
To John Robinson, Esquire .	25,000			18,000					
				40,000					
							58,000		
Between 5 January, 1782, and 30 March, 1782,									
To Sir Grey Cooper. . .	8,000								
To John Robinson, Esquire	11,000			13,860	4	2			
				19,000					
							32,860	4	2

4

AN ACCOMPT OF THE MONEY ISSUED FOR HIS MAJESTY'S SECRET AND
5TH JANUARY, 1769, AND THE

		Secret Service.			Special Service.		
		l.	*s*	*d*	*l.*	*s*	*d.*
1769							
27 January	To Grey Cooper, Esquire . . .	4,000					
17 February	To ditto	4,000					
3 March	To ditto	4,000					
10 March	To ditto	4,000					
17 March	To ditto	4,000					
14 April	To ditto	6,000					
17 April	To Thomas Bradshaw, Esquire	..			11,000		
26 May	To Grey Cooper, Esquire . .	4,000					
9 June	To ditto	..			3,477	7	6
16 June	To ditto	..			4,213	5	6
7 July	To ditto . . .	..			6,315	14	
14 July	To ditto	4,000					
25 August	To Thomas Bradshaw, Esquire .	4,000					
28 September	To Grey Cooper, Esquire	4,000					
10 November	To ditto	..			4,213	5	6
8 December	To ditto . . .	4,000					
22 December	To Thomas Bradshaw, Esquire	.			4,240		
1770							
19 January	To Grey Cooper, Esquire	4,000					
14 February	To Thomas Bradshaw, Esquire .	...			1,048		
16 February	To ditto	4,000					
9 March	To ditto	4,000					
6 April	To Milward Rowe, Esquire	4,000					
6 April	To Thomas Bradshaw, Esquire . . .	.			17,000		
8 June	To Grey Cooper, Esquire	4,000					
22 June	To ditto . . . . . ' .	4,000					
6 July	To ditto	4,000					
3 August	To ditto . . .	2,000					
17 August	To ditto	..			4,213	5	
	Borne forward	76,000			55,720	17	6

4*b*

ECIAL SERVICE TO THE PERSONS UNDERMENTIONED BETWEEN THE
1 JANUARY, 1777. VIZT.

Civil List Revenues.			Late King's Arrears			Money from Guadeloupe by C Hamilton, Esq			Revenues of Dutchy of Cornwall.			Virginia Quit Rents			Revenue of Gibraltar.			4½ per Cent		
l.	*s*	*d*	*l.*	*s*	*d*	*l.*	*s.*	*d*	*l.*	*s*	*d.*	*l.*	*s.*	*d*	*l*	*s*	*d*	*l*	*s.*	*d*
4,000																				
4,000																				
4,000																				
4,000																				
4,000																				
3,000																				
..			..						11,000											
4,000																				
			1,149	6	1	183	13	½	.						2,144	8	4½			
									.						..			4,213	5	6
									.						.			6,315	14	
4,000																				
4,000																				
4,000																				
			..									..			..			4,213	5	6
4,000																				
						..			..			4,240								
4,000																				
.						.						1,048								
4,000																				
4,000																				
4,000																				
..			..						17,000											
4,000 -																				
4,000																				
4,000																				
2,000																				
			..			.			.			.						4,213	5	
3,000			1,149	6	1	183	13	½	28,000			5,288			2,144	8	4½	18,955	10	

5

AN ACCOMPT OF THE MONEY ISSUED FOR HIS MAJESTY'S SECRET AND
5TH JANUARY, 1769, AND THE

		Secret Service			Special Service.		
		l	*s*	*d*	*l.*	*s.*	*d.*
1770	Brought forward	76,000			33,720	17	6
28 September	To Thomas Bradshaw, Esquire	..			4,213	5	
26 October	To Grey Cooper, Esquire	.			5,264	10	
26 October	To ditto	..			1,059	7	6
9 November	To ditto	4,000					
28 December	To ditto	4,000					
1771							
11 January	To ditto	4,000					
8 February	To ditto	4,000					
22 March	To ditto	4,213	5	6			
3 April	To John Robinson, Esquire . . .	..			8,700		
16 April	To ditto				4,213	5	6
22 April	To ditto				6,000		
9 May	To Grey Cooper, Esquire . . .				4,213	5	6
29 May	To John Robinson, Esq.				3,162	2	
19 July	To ditto	3,000					
16 August	To ditto	4,000					
4 October	To Grey Cooper, Esquire	4,000					
17 October	To John Robinson, Esquire . . .	..			4,000		
1 November	To Grey Cooper, Esquire	4,000					
13 December	To John Robinson, Esquire . . .	4,000					
23 December	To ditto	..			914	8	2
1772							
10 January	To Grey Cooper, Esquire . .	4,000					
5 February	To John Robinson, Esquire .	..			900		
28 February	To ditto	4,000					
13 March	To ditto	4,000					
10 April	To Grey Cooper, Esquire . . .	4,000					
16 April	To John Robinson, Esquire . . .	..			13,000		
10 June	To ditto	..			150		
19 June	To ditto	3,000					
3 July	To Grey Cooper, Esquire	2,000					
8 July	To John Robinson, Esquire . . .	..			5,000		
12 August	To Grey Cooper, Esquire	..			3,165	15	6
28 August	To John Robinson, Esquire . . .	3,000					
9 October	To Grey Cooper, Esquire	..			3,158	5	6
	Borne forward	139,213	5	6	122,835	2	2

5*b*

ECIAL SERVICE TO THE PERSONS UNDERMENTIONED BETWEEN THE
H JANUARY, 1777. VIZT.

Out of his Majesty's Civil List Revenues	Late King's Arrears.	Money from Guadeloupe C Hamilton	Revenue of Dutchy of Cornwall.	Virginia Quit Rents	Revenue of Gibraltar	4½ per Cent	Nova Scotia Quit Rents
l s d	*l s d*	*l. s d.*	*l. s. d*	*l s d*	*l s d.*	*l. s. d.*	*l s d.*
6,000	1,149 6 1	183 13 ½	28,000	5,288	2,144 8 4½	18,955 10	
..	..	..	..			4,213 5	
..	..	..		..	1,059 7 6	5,264 10	
4,000							
4,000							
4,000							
4,000							
			..	..	..	4,213 5 6	
.	..		8,700			4,213 5 6	
.		.	..	..	..		
			..	6,000		4,213 5 6	
..	..	..	..	..	..	3,162 2	
..	.	..	..	..	.		
3,000							
4,000							
4,000							
..	..	..		4,000			
4,000							
4,000							
.	.		.	.	914 8 2		
4,000							
.	.	.	..	900			
4,000							
4,000 -							
4,000							
.	..	..	13,000				
..	.	.	..	.		.	150
3,000							
2,000							
	.	..		5,000			
		.		.		3,165 15 6	
3,000							
..	..	..	..	..	..	3,158 5 6	
5,000	1,149 6 1	183 13 ½	49,700	21,188	4,118 4 ½	50,559 4 6	150

6

AN ACCOMPT OF THE MONEY ISSUED FOR HIS MAJESTY'S SECRET AND
5TH JANUARY, 1769, AND THE

		Secret Service.			Special Service.			Out of his Majesty's Civil List Revenues			Late King's Arrears.		
		l.	*s*	*d.*	*l.*	*s.*	*d.*	*l*	*s*	*d*	*l.*	*s*	*d*
1772	Brought forward . .	139,213	5	6	122,835	2	2	135,000			1,149	6	1
30 October	To John Robinson, Esquire	4,000						4,000					
16 November	To ditto				958	7	4½						
18 December	To Grey Cooper, Esquire .	2,000						2,000					
18 December	To John Robinson, Esquire	3,000						3,000					
1773													
20 January	To ditto				4,000								
22 January	To Grey Cooper, Esquire	2,000						2,000					
11 March	To ditto				3,162	2							
11 March	To John Robinson, Esquire				349								
11 March	To ditto				570								
12 March	To ditto	4,000						4,000					
1 April	To ditto				1,000								
23 April	To Grey Cooper, Esquire .				2,110	14	6						
14 May	To John Robinson, Esquire	5,000						5,000					
21 May	To ditto	5,000						5,000					
23 May	To ditto				12,800								
23 May	To ditto				4,095								
2 July	To Grey Cooper, Esquire .	4,000						4,000					
16 July	To John Robinson, Esquire	3,000						3,000					
30 July	To ditto. . . .	3,000						3,000					
20 August	To Grey Cooper, Esquire .	2,000						2,000					
22 October	To ditto .	4,000						4,000					
29 November	To John Robinson, Esquire	4,000						4,000					
1774													
7 January	To Grey Cooper, Esquire	2,000						2,000					
20 January	To John Robinson, Esquire				4,000								
21 January	To ditto	3,000						3,000					
4 February	To ditto	160											
4 March	To ditto				6,193	19	8½	6,193	19	8½			
18 March	To Grey Cooper, Esquire	2,000						2,000					
25 March	To ditto	1,000						1,000					
25 March	To John Robinson, Esquire	4,000						4,000					
6 May	To Grey Cooper, Esquire	2,000						2,000					
6 May	To John Robinson, Esquire	4,000						4,000					
13 May	To ditto . .	1,000						1,000					
	Borne forward . .	203,373	5	6	162,074	5	8½	205,193	19	8½	1,149	6	1

6*b*

PECIAL SERVICE TO THE PERSONS UNDERMENTIONED BETWEEN THE
TH JANUARY, 1777. VIZT

money from Guadeloupe per C. Hamilton.	Revenue of Duchy of Cornwall.	Virginia Quit Rents.	Revenue of Gibraltar.	4½ per Cent.	Nova Scotia Quit Rents	Georgia Quit Rents.	Sale of Lands in Georgia.	Casual Revenue of Barbadoes.
s. d.	l. s. d	l s d	l s d	l. s. d	l. s d	l s. d.	l. s d	l. s. d.
3 13 ½	49,700	21,188	4,118 4 ½	50,559 4 6	150			
			958 7 4½					
		4,000						
				3,162 2				
		349					570	
								1,000
				2,110 14 6				
	12,800							
		4,095						
		4,000						
						160		
33 13 ½	62,500	33,632	5,076 11 4½	55,832 1	150	160	570	1,000

7

An Accompt of the Money issued for His Majesty's Secret and
5th January, 1769, and the

		Secret Service.			Special Service.			Out of his Majesty's Civil List Revenues.			Late King's Arrears.		
		l.	*s*	*d.*	*l.*	*s.*	*d.*	*l.*	*s.*	*d.*	*l.*	*s.*	*d.*
1774	Brought forward . .	203,373	5	6	162,074	5	8¾	205,193	19	8½	1,149	6	1
27 May	To Grey Cooper, Esquire .	2,000			..			2,000					
27 May	To John Robinson, Esquire	3,000						3,000					
25 June	To ditto	..			2,528	12		.					
8 July	To Grey Cooper, Esquire	3,000						3,000					
8 July	To John Robinson, Esquire	5,000			..			5,000					
29 July	To ditto	5,000			..			5,000					
4 August	To ditto	..			8,000			.			..		
23 September	To Grey Cooper, Esquire .	2,000			..			2,000					
14 October	To ditto	3,000			.			3,000					
9 December	To ditto	3,000			..			3,000					
16 December	To ditto . . .	3,000			.			3,000					
1775													
27 January	To ditto . .	4,000			..			4,000					
17 February	To ditto . . .	2,000			..			2,000					
16 March	To ditto .	.			4,000			..					
26 April	To ditto	..			12,000			..					
12 May	To ditto	4,000			..			4,000					
30 June	To ditto	4,000			..			4,000					
26 August	To John Robinson, Esquire	.			280			.					
29 September	To Sir Grey Cooper. . .	2,000			..		·	2,000					
6 October	To John Robinson, Esquire	3,000			..			3,000					
27 October	To Sir Grey Cooper. . .	3,000			..			3,000					
10 November	To John Robinson, Esquire	3,000			..			3,000					
8 December	To ditto	5,000			..			5,000					
13 December	To ditto	.			3,000			.			.		
1776													
5 January	To Sir Grey Cooper. . .	4,000			..			4,000					
26 January	To John Robinson, Esquire	3,000			..			3,000					
16 February	To ditto	4,000			..			4,000					
8 March	To Sir Grey Cooper. .	2,000			..			2,000					
22 March	To John Robinson, Esquire	4,000			..			4,000					
29 March	To Sir Grey Cooper. . .	4,000			..			4,000					
	Borne forward . .	283,373	5	6	191,882	17	8¾	285,193	19	8½	1,149	6	1

7*b*

'ECIAL SERVICE TO THE PERSONS UNDERMENTIONED BETWEEN THE
'H JANUARY, 1777.   VIZT.

oney from uadeloupe per C Iamllton.	Revenue of Dutchy of Cornwall.	Virginia Qult Rents.	Revenue of Gibraltar	4½ per Cent	Nova Scotia Qult Rents.	Georgia Qult Rents	Sale of Lands in Georgia	Casual Revenue of Bar-badoes
l. s. d	*l. s. d*	*l. s. d*	*l s. d*	*l. s. d*	*l. s. d.*	*l. s. d*	*l s d*	*l. s d*
;3 13 ½	62,500	33,632	5,076 11 4¾	55,832 1	150	160	,570	1,000
.	..	2,528 12						
..	8,000							
.	.. 12,000	4,000						
.		..			280			
..	..	.3,000						
;3 13 ½	82,500	48,160 12	5,076 11 4¾	55,832 1	430	160	570	1,000

8

AN ACCOMPT OF THE MONEY ISSUED FOR HIS MAJESTY'S SECRET AND
5TH JANUARY, 1769, AND THE

		Secret Service			Special Service.			Out of his Majesty's Civil List Revenues.			Late King's Arrears.		
		l	*s*.	*d*.	*l*	*s*	*d*.	*l*.	*s*	*d*	*l*.	*s*.	*d*.
1776	Brought forward	283,373	5	6	191,882	17	8¾	285,193	19	8½	1,149	6	1
17 April	To John Robinson, Esquire		.		12,950				.				
21 June	To Sir Grey Cooper. . .	2,500				..		2,500					
28 June	To ditto	1,500				..		1,500					
5 July	To ditto	3,000				..		3,000					
23 August	To John Robinson, Esquire	3,000				. .		3,000					
25 October	To Sir Grey Cooper. . .	4,000				.		4,000					
8 November	To John Robinson, Esquire	4,000				.		4,000					
6 December	To ditto . . .	4 000				..		4,000					
		305,373	5	6	204,832	17	8¾	307,193	19	8½	1,149	6	1
		204,832	17	8¾									
		510,206	3	2¾									

8*b*

ECIAL SERVICE TO THE PERSONS UNDERMENTIONED BETWEEN THE
H JANUARY, 1777. VIZT.

ney from uadeloupe per C. amilton	Revenue of Duchy of Cornwall.	Virginia Quit Rents	Revenue of Gibraltar.	4½ per Cent.	Nova Scotia Quit Rents.	Georgia Quit Rents	Sale of Lands in Georgia.	Casual Revenue of Barbadoes
l. s. d.	*l. s d*	*l. s d*	*l s. d.*	*l. s. d.*	*l s d*	*l s d*	*l s d*	*l. s. d.*
33 13 ½	82,500	43,160 12	5,076 11 4½	55,832 1	430	160	570	1,000
	12,950							
3 13 ½	95,450	43,160 12	5,076 11 4½	55,832 1	430	160	570	1,000
							307,193 19 8½	
							1,149 6 1	
							183 13 ½	
							95,450	
							43,160 12	
							5,076 11 4½	
							55,832 1	
							430	
							160	
							570	
							1,000	
							510,206 3 2⅞	

9

AN ACCOMPT OF THE MONEY ISSUED FOR HIS MAJESTY'S SECRET AND
5TH OF JANUARY, 1777, AND

		Secret Service.			Special Service		
		l.	*s.*	*d*	*l.*	*s.*	*d*
1777							
24 January	To Sir Grey Cooper, Baronet .	4,000					
7 February	To John Robinson, Esquire .	4,000					
28 February	To ditto	4,000					
14 March	To ditto	2,000					
4 April	To ditto	2,000					
11 April	To Sir Grey Cooper, Baronet .	6,000					
9 May	To John Robinson, Esquire .	2,000					
23 May	To ditto . . .	2,000			.		
29 May	To ditto .	..			9,720		
30 May	To Sir Grey Cooper. . .	2,000					
6 June	To ditto	2,000					
18 July	To John Robinson, Esquire .	5,000					
25 July	To Sir Grey Cooper. . . .	2,000			..		
15 August	To ditto	1,000					
16 August	To John Robinson, Esquire .				3,774		8½
17 October	To ditto	5,000			..		
31 October	To ditto	5,000			..		
31 October	To Sir Grey Cooper. . .	3,000			..		
12 December	To John Robinson, Esquire . .	4,000			..		
1778							
2 January	To Sir Grey Cooper. .	2,000					
23 January	To ditto	2,000					
23 January	To John Robinson, Esquire .	5,000			..		
20 March	To ditto	5,000			.		
27 March	To ditto	..			20,000		
10 April	To Sir Grey Cooper. . . .	4,000			..		
17 April	To ditto	2,000			..		
17 April	To John Robinson, Esquire .	6,000			..		
17 April	To ditto . .	..			15,964		
	Borne forward	81,000			49,458		8½

9*b*

ECIAL SERVICES TO THE PERSONS UNDERMENTIONED BETWEEN THE
E 5TH OF JANUARY [30 MARCH, 1782].

Out of his Majesty's Civil List Revenues.			Balance Account Sir Lynch Cotton, late Receiver of Land Revenues in North Wales and Chester.			Revenue of Duchy of Cornwall.		
l.	*s.*	*d.*	*l.*	*s.*	*d.*	*l.*	*s.*	*d.*
4,000								
4,000								
4,000								
2,000								
2,000								
6,000								
2,000								
2,000								
..			..			9,720		
2,000								
2,000								
5,000								
2,000								
1,000								
..			3,774		8½			
5,000								
5,000								
3,000								
4,000								
2,000								
2,000								
5,000								
5,000								
20,000								
4,000								
2,000								
6,000								
..			..			15,964		
101,000			3,774		8½	25,684		

M

10

AN ACCOMPT OF THE MONEY ISSUED FOR HIS MAJESTY'S SECRET AND
5TH OF JANUARY, 1777, AND

		Secret Service.			Special Service.		
		l.	*s*	*d.*	*l.*	*s.*	*d.*
1778	Brought forward . . .	81,000			49,458		8½
12 June	To John Robinson, Esquire .	6,000			..		
3 July	To Sir Grey Cooper . . .	4,000			..		
2 October	To John Robinson, Esquire . .	6,000			..		
16 October	To Sir Grey Cooper	3,000			..		
3 November	To ditto	2,000			..		
25 December	To ditto	3,000			..		
1779							
5 January	To ditto	3,000			..		
12 February	To ditto	3,000			.		
19 February	To John Robinson, Esquire .	5,000			..		
26 March	To ditto	7,000			..		
3 April	To Sir Grey Cooper . . .	2,000			..		
16 April	To John Robinson, Esquire . .	..			6,640		
28 May	To ditto	6,000			..		
25 June	To Sir Grey Cooper	3,000			..		
16 July	To ditto	2,000			..		
16 July	To John Robinson, Esquire . .	5,000			..		
23 July	To ditto	..			10,000		
12 August	To ditto	5,000			..		
3 September	To ditto	6,000			..		
8 October	To ditto	6,000			..		
8 October	To Sir Grey Cooper	4,000			..		
12 November	To ditto	2,000			..		
12 November	To John Robinson, Esquire . .	6,000			..		
15 November	To ditto	..			2,000		
		170,000			68,098		8½
		68,098	8½				
		238,098	8½				

10*b*

ECIAL SERVICES TO THE PERSONS UNDERMENTIONED BETWEEN THE
E 5TH OF JANUARY [30 MARCH, 1782].

Out of his Majesty's Civil List Revenues	Balance of Account of Sir Lynch Cotton, Late Receiver of Land Revenue in North Wales and Chester.		Revenue of Duchy of Cornwall.		Revenue of Gibraltar.	
l. *s.* *d.*	*l.* *s.*	*d.*	*l.* *s.*	*d*	*l.* *s*	*d*
101,000	3,774	8½	25,684			
6,000						
4,000						
6,000						
3,000						
2,000						
3,000						
3,000	•					
3,000						
5,000						
7,000						
2,000						
..	..		6,640			
6,000						
3,000						
2,000						
5,000						
10,000						
5,000						
6,000						
6,000						
4,000						
2,000						
6,000						
..	..		.		2,000	
200,000	3,774	8½	32,324		2,000	
					32,324	
					3,774	8½
					200,000	
					238,098	8½

II

An Accompt of the Money issued for His Majesty's Secret and
5th of January, 1777, and

		Secret Service			Special Service.		
		l.	*s.*	*d.*	*l.*	*s.*	*d.*
1780	Brought forward .	170,000			68,098		8½
21 January	To Sir Grey Cooper.	2,000					
4 February	To ditto . .	3,000					
14 April	To ditto . . .	3,000					
21 April	To John Robinson, Esquire .	5,000			.		
23 June	To ditto . .	5,000			. .		
26 June	To ditto . . .	. .			8,603		
7 July	To Sir Grey Cooper. . .	4,000			.		
18 August	To John Robinson, Esquire .	5,000			.		
20 October	To Sir Grey Cooper. .	4,000			.		
10 November	To ditto . . .	2,000			.		
15 December	To ditto . . .	2.000			. .		
22 December	To John Robinson, Esquire	. .			2,900		
1781							
5 January	To Sir Grey Cooper. .	2,000			.		
16 February	To ditto	3,000			.		
16 February	To John Robinson, Esquire .	5,000			.		
14 April	To Sir Grey Cooper. .	2,000			.		
11 May	To John Robinson, Esquire .	5,000			.		
12 May	To ditto	.			15,700		
29 June	To Sir Grey Cooper. . . .	2,000			.		
6 July	To ditto	2,000			.		
13 July	To John Robinson, Esquire . ' .	5,000			.		
20 July	To Sir Grey Cooper. . . .	3,000			. .		
31 August	To John Robinson, Esquire	5,000			.		
23 October	To ditto	.			2,300		
26 October	To Sir Grey Cooper . .	3,000			. .		
16 November	To John Robinson, Esquire . .	5,000					
	Borne forward	247,000			97,601		8½
		97,601		8½			
		344,601		8½			

11*b*

'ECIAL SERVICES TO THE PERSONS UNDERMENTIONED BETWEEN THE
IE 5TH OF JANUARY [30 MARCH, 1782].

'ut of his Majesty's Civil List Revenues			Balance of Account of Sir Lynch Cotton, late Receiver of Land Revenues in North Wales and Chester			Revenue of Dutchy of Cornwall			Revenue of Gibraltar.		
l.	*s*	*d*	*l.*	*s.*	*d.*	*l.*	*s.*	*d*	*l.*	*s.*	*d.*
200,000			3,774		8½	32,324			2,000		
2,000											
3,000											
3,000											
5,000											
5,000											
..						8,603					
4,000											
5,000											
4,000											
2,000											
2,000											
.									2,900		
2,000											
3,000											
5,000											
2,000											
5,000											
..						15,000					
2,000											
2,000											
5,000											
3,000											
5,000											
.									2,300		
3,000											
5,000											
277,000			3,774		8½	56,627			7,200		
									56,627		
									3,774		8½
									277,000		
									344,601		8½

12 [1]

		Secret Service.			Special Service.		
		l.	*s.*	*d.*	*l.*	*s.*	*d.*
1782	Brought forward . .	247,000			97,601		8½
11 January	To Sir Grey Cooper . . .	4,000					
15 January	To John Robinson, Esquire.	..			2,531	4	
25 January	To ditto	5,000					
1 February	To Sir Grey Cooper .	2,000					
15 March	To ditto . . .	2,000					
22 March	To John Robinson, Esquire.	6,000					
25 March	To ditto	..			8,658		
30 March	To ditto . . .	..			2,651	2	

[1] Page 12*b* is lacking, and the next page would be numbered 18*b*, the first part of the sheet being wanting. Although Mr. Stevens insisted that the intervening pages are blank in the original book, and so he did not make facsimiles of them, it would nevertheless seem from the contents of the pages here that both the second part of sheet 12 and the first part of sheet 18 contained items in these accounts. See p. 186.

18*b*

		l.	*s.*	*d.*	*l.*	*s.*	*d*
1776	Brought forward	1,992	18	6	5,109	9	
9 February	Thomas Pratt for Thomas Flucker, including *l* 22 14 9 for fees .	322	14	9			
	Ditto for Richard Ocklom Harrison, including *l.*22 14 9 for fees	322	14	9			
8 March	Ditto for Captain Fenton, including *l.*15 17 for fees	165	17				
	Ditto for Dr. Moffatt, including *l.*13 7 for fees	113	7				
15 March	Ditto for ditto, including *l.*23 11 for fees	323	11				
29 March	Ditto for Samuel Porter, including *l.*23 10 for fees	323	10				
6 April	Ditto for David Ingersoll, *l.*100 ⎫ Ditto for George Davidson *l.*50 ⎬ For fees *l.*15 17 ⎭	165	17				
	Ditto for Walter Whitaker, including *l.*18 8 for fees . .	218	8				
26 April	Ditto for Daniel Still *l.*140 ⎫ Ditto for John Trentbrooke *l.*50 ⎬ For fees *l.*17 17 6 ⎭	207	17	6			
3 May	Ditto for John Mercer, including *l.*28 12 for fees	428	12				
	Ditto for Walter Whitaker, including *l* 33 16 for fees . . .	533	16				
28 June	Ditto for John Vernon, including *l.*16 for fees . . .	168	10				
	Ditto for J. Lloyd, including *l.*18 4 for fees	213	16				
5 July	Ditto to be paid over to sundry persons, including *l.*264 12 for fees	5,264	12				
26 July	Milward Rowe, to be paid over to sundry persons, including *l.*264 15 for fees	5,264	15				
9 August	Ditto for ditto, including *l.*264 12 for fees	5,264	12				
13 December	Ditto for ditto, including *l.*264 12 for fees	5,264	12				
					26,560		6
					31,669	9	6

19

		l.	*s.*	*d.*	*l.*	*s.*	*d.*
	Brought forward .				31,669	9	6
	In the year ended 5th January, 1778						
1777							
11 April	M. Rowe, Esq. for John						
	Vernon . . . *l.*604						
	Fees . . 39 2 6						
		643	2	6			
	Ditto for American Sufferers .	5,264	12				
9 May	Ditto for ditto .	5,264	12				
27 June	Ditto for ditto . .	5,264	12				
11 July	Ditto for ditto . .	15,777	8				
18 July	Ditto for ditto	5,264	12				
15 August	Ditto for ditto	5,264	12				
19 September	Ditto for ditto	10,521	6	6			
7 November	Ditto for ditto	5,264	12				
					58,529	9	
	In the year ended 5th January, 1779						
1778							
9 January	M. Rowe, Esq. for American Suf-						
	ferers	5,264	12				
16 January	Ditto for ditto	5,264	12				
6 February	Ditto for ditto . . .	5,264	12				
13 February	Ditto for ditto . . .	5,264	12				
10 April	Ditto for ditto	5,264	12				
17 April	Ditto for ditto . . .	5,264	12				
24 April	Ditto for ditto . . .	5,264	12				
3 July	Ditto for ditto . . .	5,264	12				
10 July	Ditto for ditto .	5,264	12				
17 July	Ditto for ditto . .	5,264	12				
21 August	Ditto for ditto .	5,264	12				
16 October	Ditto for ditto .	5,264	12				
11 December	Ditto for ditto . .	5,264	12				
					68,439	16	
	In the year ended 5th January, 1780						
1779							
22 January	M. Rowe, Esq. for American Suf-						
	ferers . .	10,529	4				
5 March	Ditto for ditto .	5,264	12				
9 April	Ditto for ditto . .	5,264	12				
21 May	Ditto for ditto .	5,264	12				
2 July	Ditto for ditto .	5,264	12				
23 July	Ditto for ditto . . .	5,264	12				
20 August	Ditto for ditto .	5,264	12				
17 September	Ditto for ditto . .	5,264	12				
15 October	Ditto for ditto .	5,264	12				
12 November	Ditto for ditto .	5,264	12				
					57,910	12	
					216,549	6	6

19*b*

		l.	*s*	*d.*	*l.*	*s*	*d.*
	Brought forward . . .				216,549	6	6
	In the year ended 5 January, 1781						
1780							
14 January	To M. Rowe, Esquire, for American Sufferers . . .	5,264	12				
21 January	Ditto for ditto	5,264	12				
25 February	Ditto for ditto	5,264	12				
21 April	Ditto for ditto	5,264	12				
28 April	Ditto for ditto	5,264	12				
14 July	Ditto for ditto	5,264	12				
21 July	Ditto for ditto	5,264	12				
4 August	Ditto for ditto	5,264	12				
18 August	Ditto for ditto	5,264	12				
25 September	Ditto for ditto	5,264	12				
20 October	Ditto for ditto	5,264	12				
17 November 2,764 12 } Ditto for ditto . . 24 November 2,500 }		5,264	12				
					63,175	4	
	In the year ended 5th January, 1782						
1781							
12 January	To M Rowe, Esq. for American Sufferers . .	5,264	12				
19 January	Ditto for ditto	5,264	12				
16 February	Ditto for ditto	5,264	12				
14 April	Ditto for ditto	5,264	12				
20 April	Ditto for ditto . .	5,264	12				
18 May	Ditto for ditto . . .	5,264	12				
1 June	Ditto for ditto	5,264	12				
22 June	Ditto for ditto	5,264	12				
3 August	Ditto for ditto	5,264	12				
17 August	Ditto for ditto	5,264	12				
31 August	Ditto for ditto	5,264	12				
7 September	Ditto for ditto	5,264	12				
26 October	Ditto for ditto	5,264	12				
					68,439	16	
	In the year ended 5th January, 1783						
1782							
18 January	To M. Rowe, Esq. for American Sufferers . . .	5,264	12				
25 January	Ditto for ditto . . .	5,264	12				
8 March	Ditto for ditto . . .	5,264	12[1]				

[1] The book is thus incomplete ; the final totals were not taken.

The following is a list of receipts given at St. James's,Westminster, to John Robinson by George III for " secret and special services " between April, 1771, and March 25, 1782, covering practically the entire period of Robinson's term as Secretary to the Treasury. The list was compiled by Mr. Stevens, from the receipts preserved by Robinson The date in the first column is that of the warrant or order which was Robinson's authority for issuing the money; that in the last column is the date of the king's receipt to Robinson. The second column indicates the several sums issued, and the third column the sources from which the money was drawn.

GEORGE III ; RECEIPTS TO JOHN ROBINSON, 1771–82.

SECRET AND SPECIAL SERVICES.

Date of order or warrant	Amount.			From what sources drawn	Date of King's receipt
1771	*l.*	*s.*	*d.*		1771
3 April	8,700			Revenues of Duchy of Cornwall	3 April
22 April	6,000			Virginia Quit Rents	23 April
29 May	3,162			Revenues of 4½ p.c.	30 May
17 July	3,000			Civil List Revenue	17 July
15 August	4,000			Civil List Revenue	15 August
17 October	4,000			Virginia Quit Rents	19 October
11 December	1,000			By representatives of Sir Humphrey Howorth (Land revenue North Wales)	12 December
12 December	4,000			Civil List Revenue	12 December
23 December	914	8	2	Gibraltar Revenues	23 December
1772					1772
4 February	900			Virginia Quit Rents	5 February
20 February	4,000			Civil List Revenue	20 February
12 March	4,000			Civil List Revenues	12 March
16 April	13,000			Revenue of Duchy of Cornwall	22 April
10 June	150			Revenue of Nova Scotia	11 June
11 June	3,000			Civil List Revenue	12 June
8 July	5,000			Virginia Quit Rents	9 July
24 August	3,000			Civil List Revenue	26 August
23 October	4,000			Civil List Revenue	24 October
16 November	958	7	4¼	Gibraltar Revenues	16 November
12 December	3,000			Civil List Revenue	12 December
1773					1773
20 January	4,000			Virginia Quit Rents	21 January
11 March	349			Virginia Quit Rents	12 March
11 March	570			Sales of Lands in Georgia	12 March

GEORGE III; RECEIPTS TO JOHN ROBINSON, 1771–82.
SECRET AND SPECIAL SERVICES—*continued.*

Date of order or warrant.	Amount.			From what sources drawn.	Date of King's receipt.
	l.	s.	d.		
11 March	4,000			Civil List Revenue	12 March
31 March	1,000			Casual Revenues in Barbadoes	1 April
(Date¹ when money was issued to Messrs. Forster)					
11 June (1772)	1,700			Repaid by Messrs. Forster	8 May
13 May	5,000			Civil List Revenue	13 May
20 May	5,000			Civil List Revenue	22 May
23 May	12,800			Revenue of Duchy of Cornwall	23 May
23 May	4,095			Virginia Quit Rents	24 May
14 June	246			Virginia Quit Rents	15 June
19 June	3,000			Civil List Revenue	23 July
30 July	3,000			Civil List Revenue	31 July
19 November	4,000			Civil List Revenue	20 November
1774					1774
20 January	4,000			Virginia Quit Rents	20 January
11 January	3,000			Civil List Revenue	21 January
4 February	160			Georgia Quit Rents	5 February
26 February	4,000			Civil List Revenue	26 March
2 March	6,193	19	8½	Civil List Revenue	4 March
4 May	5,000			Civil List Revenue	17 May
20 May	3,000			Civil List Revenue	23 May
25 June	2,528	12		Virginia Quit Rents	27 June
29 June	5,000			Civil List Revenue	6 July
21 July	5,000			Civil List Revenue	28 July
4 August	8,000			Revenue of the Duchy of Cornwall	8 August
1775					1775
18 August	280			Nova Scotia Quit Rents	19 August
7 September	3,000			Civil List Revenue	10 October
2 November	3,000			Civil List Revenue	6 November
7 December	5,000			Civil List Revenue	7 December
13 December	3,000			Virginia Quit Rents	16 December
13 December	3,000			Virginia Quit Rents	16 December
1776					1776
12 January	3,000			Civil List Revenue	25 January
8 February	4,000			Civil List Revenue	12 February
18 March	4,000			Civil List Revenue	21 March
17 April	12,950			Revenue of the Duchy of Cornwall	2 May

¹ Mr Stevens inserted a pencilled note saying that this sum was " first issued for the discovery of the South Pole "

GEORGE III; RECEIPTS TO JOHN ROBINSON, 1771–82
SECRET AND SPECIAL SERVICES—*continued.*

Date of order or warrant.	Amount.			From what sources drawn	Date of King's receipt.
	l	*s.*	*d*		
20 August	3,000			Civil List Revenue	22 August
6 November	4,000			Civil List Revenue	8 November
4 December 1777	4,000			Civil List Revenue	5 December 1777
13 March	4,000			Civil List Revenue	15 March
3 May	4,000			Civil List Revenue	5 May
29 May	9,720			Revenue of the Duchy of Cornwall	5 June
17 July	5,000			Civil List Revenue	19 July
16 August	3,774	0	8½	Land Revenue of North Wales	19 August
8 October	5,000			Civil List Revenue	19 October
23 October	5,000			Civil List Revenue	30 October
4 December 1778	4,000			Civil List Revenue	6 December 1778
19 January	5,000			Civil List Revenue	22 January
12 March	5,000			Civil List Revenue	14 March
18 March	20,000			Civil List Revenue	25 March
10 April	6,000			Civil List Revenue	11 April
16 April	15,964			Revenue of the Duchy of Cornwall	17 April
3 June	6,000			Civil List Revenue	5 June
26 September	6,000			Civil List Revenue	29 September
28 September 1779	6,000			Civil List Revenue	2 October 1779
16 February	5,000			Civil List Revenue	18 February
23 March	7,000			Civil List Revenue	25 March
16 April	6,640			Revenue of the Duchy of Cornwall	17 April
21 May	6,000			Civil List Revenue	25 May
12 July	5,000			Civil List Revenue	14 July
20 July	10,000			Civil List Revenue	23 July
29 July	5,000			Civil List Revenue	31 July
26 August	6,000			Civil List Revenue	30 August
28 September	6,000			Civil List Revenue	4 October
8 November	6,000			Civil List Revenue	12 November
15 November	2,000			Gibraltar Revenues	18 November 1780
16 November 1780	25,000			Civil List Revenue	21 January
10 April	5,000			Civil List Revenue	18 April
10 April	5,000			Civil List Revenue	19 April

GEORGE III; RECEIPTS TO JOHN ROBINSON, 1771–82
SECRET AND SPECIAL SERVICES—*continued.*

Date of order or warrant	Amount			From what sources drawn	Date of King's receipt
	l.	*s.*	*d*		
16 June	5,000			Civil List Revenue	19 June
26 June	8,603			Revenue of the Duchy of Cornwall	30 June
8 August	5,000			Civil List Revenue	18 August
22 December 1781	2,900			Gibraltar Revenues	29 December 1781
14 February	5,000			Civil List Revenue	15 February
3 May	5,000			Civil List Revenue	5 May
11 July	5,000			Civil List Revenue	13 July
20 August	5,000			Civil List Revenue	21 August
23 October	2,300			Gibraltar Revenues	31 October
9 November 1782	5,000			Civil List Revenue	16 November 1782
10 January	5,000			Civil List Revenue	21 January
15 January	2,531	4		Civil List Revenue	27 February
27 January	2,514	5	2	Civil List Revenue	26 March
28 February	6,000			Civil List Revenue	21 March
25 March	8,658			Revenue of the Duchy of Cornwall	27 March

APPENDIX I

The following letters, selected from a much larger number written by Robinson to Henry Nevill and transcribed by Mr. Stevens, are appended here because they illustrate the prevailing methods of establishing an interest in a close borough and of obtaining election from a county. The correspondence pertaining to the steps incidental to the choice of Nevill as member for Monmouthshire was occasioned by the death of John Hanbury, returned for the county April 8, 1784, a few days after his election. Nevill, who had meditated standing for election in the general election, now determined to stand to succeed the deceased member. The first letter in this group is included because it contains information concerning the intention of the new administration in 1783 to dissolve parliament soon after taking office.

1783, December 22 —John Robinson to Henry Nevill   " I wrote the inclosed letter to you thinking you might have come to town, but, finding that you have not, I send it to you. All is yet confusion ; Lord Temple has resigned the seals of Secretary of State An address to the throne has this night passed the House of Commons to desire the King would not prorogue or dissolve Parliament. Certainly, therefore, you need not *yet* come again to town on such an account. You shall hear more from me the moment I can say more of anything material ; but you shall see me as soon as it is possibly in my power to return home. Remember me most affectionately to all the family."

1784, January 21 —Syon Hill.   John Robinson's draft of a letter to be written to Mr. John Hanbury, the sitting member for Monmouthshire, by Henry Nevill, inclosed in a letter to Nevill.   " The report of a dissolution of parliament is again revived with more confidence and assertions that it will soon happen. The former

175

reports would, I can have no doubt, reach you, and you will, I conclude, have formed your resolutions upon this subject. Some accounts say you have, from the state of your health, thoughts of declining to represent the county, others that you will again offer yourself Under these circumstances I have been obligingly thought of as a candidate. I hope you will believe that it is my sincerest wish in your absence not to do anything that shall appear to be acting unkindly or improperly to you, an old friend of my family. I shall be very much obliged to you, therefore, for a candid information of your sentiments and wishes on this occasion, and I shall lay them before my friends. It will give me pleasure if the opinions of my friends should coincide with yours If your resolution should be at present to decline the trouble of a parliamentary attendance, I shall feel myself much obliged to you for your approbation and support of my standing, and if you should determine to stand, be assured that it will be with reluctance I give you trouble, should my friends after consideration think I ought to offer myself to the county of Monmouth."

1784, April 17.—Harwich   John Robinson to Henry Nevill. " Your letter of yesterday came to me by express very early this morning I have been in doubt all this day whether I should not come up to town to-morrow on East India business in consequence of letters I have received from Atkinson, which has made me delay a little writing to you, as well as that I would not have you all disturbed in the night by the express. You have acted, my Dear Henry, in my opinion, perfectly right in the steps you have taken. The first thing is, What does your father say ? What are his wishes ? The next, What says his grace of Beaufort ? To *know* *their sentiments*, you have taken the proper steps ; you will before this have heard your father's. If he approves your submitting yourself to stand for the county, if agreeable to the gentlemen, I think it would be right for you to call on Sir Charles Gould to thank him for the intelligence he had given you, to say that you had seen Lord Abergavenny, who approved of your offering yourself to the county if it was agreeable to the gentlemen to elect you, that you had wrote to the Duke of Beaufort to know his sentiments, and that you would or had wrote (as the fact is when you see him), to Mr. Morgan and should be extremely happy if you were so fortunate as to meet with their concurrence and support, thinking yourself now at liberty to ask it, which you did not before in Mr. Hanbury's life, as he had told you in his letter he wished to continue in for the county, which you would not obstruct. Your letter to Mr. Morgan should, I think, run to the following effect : That on the report of Mr. Hanbury's intention to quit his seat for the county of Monmouth on account of his health a wish that you would offer yourself had been mentioned to you by many gentlemen ; that you did not think it right to give attention to such proposals until you knew Mr. Hanbury's sentiments, who had been long connected with your family, and therefore you wrote to him on the occasion, and receiving his answer that he wished to continue to represent the county you had entirely dropped the thoughts of it, but that now Mr. Hanbury was no more you took the liberty to address them on the subject, as you had the Duke of Beaufort, and should esteem yourself happy if you could be honoured with their approbation and support, and the rest of the gentlemen of the county ; and that if so you would immediately either attend a public meeting for the nomination of a proper person to be a candidate on this occasion or take such measures as should be most proper This done, I should think no other step could with propriety be taken until it was determined whether the sheriff should be requested to hold a public meeting for the nomination or not, except that Morgan and Kinsey, your father's agents, and your private friends should let it be known that you shall be happy to have the honour to represent them if it should be agreeable to the gentlemen of the county and that in this case you would quit your seat at Seaforth. But I ask your pardon in this last paragraph. I have recollected myself, and I submit to *you* whether when you write to Mr. *Morgans,* as above mentioned, you should not also write to *Mr. Williams.* Of this you will best judge, and act as you see right. No steps can be taken on this vacancy but calling a meeting for a nomination of a candidate, or, if an opposition, a canvass, until two or three days after the meeting of Parliament at the very soonest, because no writs can be moved until the Speaker is chose and approved. You will, therefore, have time enough to take these preliminary steps and to arrange matters so as that you may vacate your present seat, being secure of Monmouthshire. Under these circumstances, it appears to me to be best for me to stay here until you hear from the Duke of Beaufort in order that I may be ready to be with you when a more active situation may come on, and in this time preparing so that I might come off at a moment's notice, for by this means

N

I shall be more at liberty than if I was to come up *now* and in a few days again be under the absolute necessity of coming hither. I shall, therefore, my Dear Henry, wait for orders and information from you, to hear your father's sentiments and the Duke of Beaufort's, etc., etc., but be ready to come up on very short notice. Be so good, therefore, if you *have occasion* to write to me by express, to send your letter to me with a card to Mr. Rose, through whose hands this comes, and he will forward it to me. But you know the post comes every night but Sunday night, and we have the letters the next evening.

"I have now nothing to add on this subject, my Dear Henry, but that I should most certainly be happy to see you represent *Monmouthshire* sooner than *Seaforth*, for all the various reasons we have so often talked over, as more honourable for you and more proper, and you may be assured that I will exert myself and do everything which I can do to promote it, short of an expensive contest, which from your altered situation (having now got a seat, although without our privity and to our surprize, yet still it is a seat and, I hope, a sure one), does not seem necessary. Pray tell Mrs R[obinson] that I received both hers and the pacquets of letters, etc , as I did those you sent me with your express, for which accept my best thanks I am extremely happy to hear pleasing accounts of all your healths. Remember me affectionately to them all."

1784, April 25.—Harwich. John Robinson to Henry Nevill "I have but time, my dear Henry, to say a very few words to you to-day, to save this post, and to acknowledge dear Mary's letter, which I received last night. I was happy to hear of your arrival back safe and well and from her letter that everything goes well as to Monmouthshire. I send you inclosed a very civil letter which I have received from Mr. Hanbury and which I have as civilly acknowledged and thanked him for. Mary tells me you have had one also. You have, I hope, wrote to him if you did not see him. *Your Morgan* also wrote to me the inclosed, which I have likewise answered The Duke's advice to go to the *Morgans* was perfectly well judged, and I am very glad that they have behaved so. I think it will prevent all opposition, for of all the candidates named, I should have feared Mr. H. Williams, I think, the most. I hope Sir S[amuel ?] F[ludyer ?] will also give way to you Pray write to *Lord Oxford*. I am vastly sorry that I cannot instantly return, having an election into the corporation about the middle of the week which will take up two days. But I trust to leave this place by this day sen'night pretty clear of all things. I have wrote to Mr. Rose to consult Mr. Hatsell and other people in town about the election, but I fear it is not possible to have it again for Monmouthshire before the parliament meets and before a new writ shall be issued Thank dear Mary for her letter ; you shall hear more from me tomorrow. This will be forwarded to you by Mr. Rose, as it will come sooner to you, and he will write to you the result of his inquiries."

1784, April 27.—Harwich, Guildhall, near 1 p m John Robinson to Henry Nevill "I intended to have wrote to you very fully by this day's post in answer to your letter to me and also to have thanked my dear Mary for hers, but I have been engaged very busily in corporation matters, have been here in court since ten o'clock and am still kept here, so that I fear to lose the post. I therefore scrawl this to account to you for my silence and just to mention that I hope you will think it right to call on Mr. Rigby to solicit his interest for you in Monmouthshire. For, whatever has passed between him and me relative to this place, yet you will recollect how very handsomely he behaved to you when it was first thought of your standing and the strong manner he wrote to Mr. Rogers on it. Besides probably he may not dislike having such an opportunity as this by way of opening ground for a resignation, which considering *all things* and the neighbours we must be, is certainly not undesirable. We are in court to-day about opening the new market and completing it and about *Hughson's* resignation, which should have *come before* the election you will recollect, but is now come and this moment accept[ed]. I must get a friend and sure person elected in his room and then this will be one more *True Ball*. Indeed I could, if vacancies, elect many more staunch friends, and the more I see of them the more truly I can say so, and it will be the happiness of my life, be assured, my dear Henry, to see the fair prospect of leaving to you and yours full weight here."

1784, May 1.—Harwich. John Robinson to Henry Nevill. " Many, many thanks to you, my dear Henry, for your letter of the 29th past, which as it contained such two pieces of news, your father's promotion in the peerage and your success in your canvass for Monmouthshire, which are so agreeable to you, believe me came doubly welcome to me. I most heartily and sincerely congratulate you on them, and be assured that whatever conduces to your and your family's happiness will ever give to me the most heartfelt satisfaction   For, believe me, that is the main object of the remaining part of my life and guides all my actions . . .   I am glad you solicited Mr Rigby , it would have seemed too particular if you had not, and it is pleasing he was so civil to you   Your reception on the canvass is very flattering, and I think with your other friends it will be right for you to go into Monmouthshire again by and by, but then it should *not be*, I think, *too soon* or *long* before the election can be had, because if so you must go about canvassing personally and in all the villages and towns. .   .   I apprized you by dear Mary that it is impossible to have the Monmouthshire election but upon a *new writ* after the parliament meets, and I desired to know if there was anything which I can do to assist you, for in that case everything shall give way."

APPENDIX II

In the letter to the Marquess of Abergavenny dated July 7, 1892, appended here in large part, Mr. Stevens made a report to their owner on the nature of the material he had found in the papers entrusted to him for examination. This letter is interesting both because of its reference to papers of which Mr. Stevens made no copies and because it illustrates the purposes and methods of work of the one to whom we are indebted for the copying of the papers contained in this volume.

In discharge of the promise to give your Lordship my notions of the biographical and historical value of the John Robinson papers in box H, which your Lordship was so good as to entrust to me, and which I herewith return, I have pleasure in submitting the following report :—

The Royal Commission on Historical Manuscripts, in the Appendix to the Tenth Report, issued in 1887, gives a descriptive list of a portion of the exceedingly interesting and valuable papers in the muniment room at Eridge Castle. At the end of that Appendix it is stated that " in another box are several bundles of papers and tabular statements shewing the state of political parties in Parliament and the probable results of general elections, 1772–1782 "

I have had great pleasure in perusing the papers in box H. They are now sorted into 18 bundles which I think may be briefly classified under three heads : (A) The papers in bundles 1 to 10, relative to political parties and results of elections referred to in the Report of the Royal Commission, with various Treasury accounts and statements, a most valuable part of which relate to the Secret Service of George III. (B) Miscellaneous, in bundles 11 to 14. (C) Family and private papers, in bundles 15 to 18.

It should be noted that many of these papers are correlative with and explanatory of those given in the Appendix to the Royal Commission Report   Thus, the letter from Mr. Robinson, No. 547, on p. 64, explains the existence of the states and political information contained in the packet marked 5 in this Box H.

I now proceed to describe the papers more particularly, in the order already indicated, and for more ready reference I have marked ten parcels " A " and have numbered them respectively from 1 to 10   Nos. 1 to 5 contain a number of " States " of political parties in Parliament ;   " States " of Boroughs in England, Wales, and Scotland ; Lists of Members in both Houses holding offices ; List of Offices tenable by members ; " States " of divisions, as on the Royal Marriage Bill in 1772 ; Lists of candidates, calculations, and memoranda.

Most of these are not dated, but they are really within the years 1772 to 1784, and they have special reference to the changes of governnent in 1772, in 1782, and in 1783.   The information they contain with regard to the methods pursued to secure the election of members favourable to Administration throws a vivid light on the politics of that, and perhaps of the present time.

In these Parliamentary " States " members are classed under several heads, as :   " Pro present " ;   " Pro absent " ;   " Pro abroad " ;   " Hopeful present " ;   " Hopeful absent " ;   " Doubtful present " ;   " Doubtful absent " ,   " Con present " ;   " Con absent " ; and " Con abroad."   The " States " of seats in the open and close boroughs are generally accompanied by remarks in the handwriting of Mr Robinson.   These remarks render the reports of double value, as they contain details of local history never known or published.   A few examples may shew their tenor.   In a " State " of open English boroughs, Mr. Robinson remarks, with respect to Hythe, that " with the support of Government the present members will make their election good here again ; and they deserve it, for they are very steady, and always well inclined to support Government, and may as such be classed Pro."   Sandwich is called a " Borough of Contests," and there are curious notes regarding it. Of Stockbridge, it is said, " This borough requires attention and management, which may make an alteration very material in it, both in the present and future Parliaments ; but in the present state of things, it is in both cases classed *against*."   Again with regard to Bristol, Mr Robinson says, " the present members for this place would stand the best chance of being again elected, though an opposition may arise, promoted by Mr. Burke's friends ; and being aided by Government these two gentlemen if elected would certainly be at least *hopeful* if not entirely *for* administration." Further on, in the same paper, we find the following remarks about Shoreham, " This place is now very open, but yet Government with management have considerable weight there, notwithstanding it being so laid open The two Gentlemen who now represent this place are well inclined and rather attached to Government , with civility they may be made steady and with fairness may be classed very hopeful in either event."

A letter from Mr. Robinson to Lord [Shelburne] dated August, 1782, and headed " most private " is accompanied by a " state " of the political sentiments of the House of Commons in " the present juncture." One entry may be quoted, referring to Charles Morgan, the candidate for Breconshire : " he is independent and desirous of peace, a friend to the constitution, a supporter of the old government in most cases. Had some family connections with the Cavendishes, yet may be hopeful. However, considering all circumstances, classed doubtful as safest."

A paper presented by a Mr Halliday to Mr Robinson on December 17, 1781, speaks for itself. It proposes that in order to prevent a contested election taking place at Taunton the sum of 500*l* be given to the silk manufacture in that town ; 300*l*. towards preserving the woollen manufacture now on its decline ; 29 shillings each to 250 poor persons who have a right to vote at an election, and 105*l*. for a public dinner after the election, and a piece of plate to the Mayor

In packet No 4 labelled, " Parliamentary—To be gone through and destroyed," we find a " list of persons with [the Administration] before, who changed." " Persons who were hopeful " who now came and voted against. " Persons who were said not to go the length with them, but who did vote with them as before " " Persons who went away." " Persons who staid away." " New Persons who did not vote before that we now got up and were with us." " New Persons that opposition got up and voted against us " " Pros that could not be got " " Cons that could not be got." These headings are sufficient to shew that no trouble or pains were spared to secure votes and also to get at an accurate state of parties.

In Packet No. 5, several very useful papers may be mentioned, such as, " list of close seats and persons fixed upon to fill them ; the same for open seats." " A state of the number of vacancies expected and of the number of candidates to supply them." " List of seats reckoned certain for money." A paper in Mr. Robinson's handwriting headed, " Private Memorandums and General Remarks," gives an exceptional amount of information with reference to the parliamentary state of boroughs and their situation in 178[3-4] on a change in the administration and Mr Pitt's coming into office. Members and places are divided into various classes ; those in the first class are described as " friends, close or under decisive influence " ; those in the second " will require *some* attention, although not so particular attention, as those *first classed* " ; the third class " may be had for money," etc

We are informed that this classing of members was sketched out at several meetings held at the house of Lord Advocate Dundas in Leicester Square, with a calculation of the money wanted for seats, which Mr Robinson says he " always disapproved, and thought very wrong " In this bundle are several letters from Mr. George Rose of the Treasury to Mr Robinson ranging in date from 1784 to 1789 They shew the active part taken by Mr Rose in the elections. He appears to have been very instrumental in " conversing with " and " managing " members. The following passages from two of his letters give a fair idea of their general nature · March 29, 1784, Duke Street, Westminster, " I am rejoiced at your last accounts of Harwich which make me tolerably comfortable on that subject , Mr Arden still thinks it desirable to have a counsel down with you, he has therefore spoke with Mr. Cowper who will be with you on Wednesday evening or Thursday morning ; he must however have 100 Guineas, which is a serious sum, if Mr. Rigby does not come forward that may be saved."

On the first of April he writes to Mr. Robinson, " this business of Ipswich is a perplexing one Mr. Middleton had encouragement given him at a time when he thought the Corporation would have been reconciled to him, which Cornwall gave great expectations of If he has no chance it is a pity that Wollaston should be irritated and made an enemy, at the same time faith must be kept with Middleton. I depend upon your prudence and discretion to manage · that and to act as you shall judge proper."

No. 6, a packet quaintly endorsed : " Treasury Papers and Accounts which may be of very essential use to a Man of business to at times look into for useful Information." These are accounts of the extra revenues applied to the Secret and other services from 1761 to 1777 , of the monies issued for Secret and Special Service from 1752 to 1768 and from 1769 to 1777 ; account of the Debt of the Civil List ; and of the charge for foreign ministers.

These Manuscripts on the Secret Service shew in all cases the source from which the funds are derived, by whom authorized, by whom expended, through whose hands they passed, to whom, or for what general purposes they were paid.

No. 7. The most valuable, however, of the papers in this box are the 103 receipts given by George III to Mr. Robinson for divers sums of money amounting to 506,261l 17s. 1$\frac{1}{4}d$ received for secret and special services It is singular indeed that these documents should have survived for more than a century.   Their very existence might well have been doubted, and the discovery of this bundle among your Lordship's Manuscripts is of high importance.

These receipts range in date from April, 1771, to March, 1782. Each of them has the sign manual of George III at the head, and the King's signature in initials at the foot. All, too, are counter-signed by Lord North. They give the date of the warrant for obtaining the money and the place where the receipt was given by the King. They also shew the funds from which the money was drawn, the principal of these being, the Revenue of the Duchy of Cornwall, the Virginian Quit Rents, Revenues of 4$\frac{1}{2}$ per cent , Civil List Revenues, Gibraltar Revenues, Nova Scotia Quit Rents, Sales of Lands in Georgia, Casual Revenues in Barbadoes, repaid by Messrs Foster from money at first issued for the discovery of the South Pole, Georgia Quit Rents, North Wales Land Revenue, and divers sums issued at the Receipt of the Exchequer Apart from the remarkable information disclosed by these papers, a particular interest attaches to them from the fact that they are the only docu-ments of the kind, bearing the signature of George III, known to be extant.   They are in an admirable state of preservation

No. 8. Treasury accounts of a most interesting character Amongst them are : " A Most Private State " of the money paid by the King to Lord North for election expenses January, 1778, to March, 1781, amounting to 40,000l. from the King and 30,010l. 17s. from other sources, together making 70,010l 17s. ; Receipts of Messrs. Drummond for most of the same and various memoranda as to the numbers of the notes, etc. ; His Majesty's

private election account from 1779 to April, 1782, shewing the
boroughs on whose accounts the various sums were paid ; also a
tabulated statement of the Payments for His Majesty's Civil Government and for the support and maintenance of his Majesty and the
Royal Family, 1769–1777, distinguishing each year.

No 9. Attention must be drawn to " the little red book," a small
red morocco volume, faded and rotten, which is supplementary to
the foregoing receipts, and contains an account of the money issued
for His Majesty's Secret and Special Service to the persons therein
mentioned from January, 1769, to January, 1782. The sums
entered as issued to Mr. John Robinson agree generally with the
receipts previously noted. Among the other persons to whom
this Secret Service money was issued are Sir Grey Cooper and
Thomas Bradshaw This account comprises 24 leaves of the
book. Further on is an account of the monies paid for the relief
and benefit of sundry Americans, officers and others, who suffered
for their attachment to His Majesty's government. This account
is rendered on four leaves ; the remainder of the book is blank.

No 10. A packet of curious and unexplained correspondence in
1778 marked by Mr Robinson, " June and July. Some Papers on
a Secret Service with Lord North, Mr. Wedderburn, Attorney
General, Mr. Pulteney, and Mr. Whately transacted by me by
Lord North's Special orders. Purpose most secret and confidential
J R. All settled by Lord North's Orders " The earliest dated
paper is a letter from Messrs Drummond, bankers, transmitting
notes for 20,000l. for Mr Robinson's draft, which notes were
instantly sent to Mr. Wedderburn " on the trust settled in him and
in Mr. Pulteney by Lord North's order." Three months later
Wedderburn begs to " be discharged of his trust in the money paid
in to Mr. Whately's and invested in the subscription," as apparently
also does Mr. Pulteney. Statements and letters relative to cash,
scrip, and sale of omnium follow, ending with a receipt from Mr.
Robinson, July 24, for the same sum of 20,000l. With this subject
incidentally occur somewhat heated references to a certain account
for 300l in which Mr. Pulteney was concerned. In connection
with this, Mr Robinson had used the word " expenses," and to him
Mr Pulteney writes . " I must set you right in another point , you
suppose that the other matter relates to expences ; now I wish you
to understand that I neither claim nor will accept of any expences
incurred by myself ; the money is for another purpose, and Lord

North knows that to be the case " Mr. Robinson replies on the 30th, " I was very sensible when I made use of the word *expences* that the sum to be paid was not for *your* expences, but what was given by you to another person for certain Expences, and therefore I am sorry you should apprehend I meant the word as applicable to you, for it certainly was not." He goes on to explain that Lord North's orders concerning the other matter did not refer to Pulteney either, and finishes by hoping that these two things are set right to his satisfaction. Perhaps this matter of the 300*l.* has reference to Mr. Pulteney's journey to Paris in the spring of 1778 to discuss informally with Dr. Franklin the means of negotiating peace with the Americans. See my Facsimile (No. 68) of Pulteney's Memoranda perused by His Majesty's Commissioners, Carlisle, Eden, and Johnstone, on board the " Trident " on their way to America to negotiate peace.

With reference to the main transaction, that of the 20,000*l.*, of this packet of papers, it is curious to note the coincidence of the amount given by the King to Lord North for the purpose of paying his debts.

In packet No. 7 amongst the King's receipts to Mr. Robinson is found one dated March 18, 1778, for this same amount, 20,000*l.*, as issued to special service.

B. MISCELLANEOUS.

Packets 11 *to* 14.

No. 11. Copy of a letter from Brigadier [Simon] Fraser dated from the Camp at Skeensborough on Wood Creek, July 13, 1777, containing the movements of Burgoyne's ill-fated expedition up to that date. Also copies of intelligence, etc., all much discoloured and very rotten.

The letter from General Fraser gives a detailed account of the operations of the campaign up to that date. Burgoyne arrived at Quebec May 6; his appearance a *coup de foudre* to Carleton ; Carleton a proud, narrow-minded man, surrounded by flatterers ; starting of the advanced corps, on the 29th of May ; general rendez-vous to be at Cumberland Head on Lake Champlain ; Fraser asks and receives permission to take post on the R. Bouquet ; information as to the environs of Ticonderoga and Mt. Independence obtained from a settler, James Macintosh ; details of various movements from the 16th to 25th June ; on the 26th the whole army at Crown Point ; on the 1st July Fraser moved the advanced corps to Three Mile Point ; conversation between Burgoyne, Phillips, and Fraser about future operations for reducing the lines, 2nd July ; Captain Fraser with Canadians and Indians sent forward on 4th July ; Indians drunk and very irregular ; copy of letter written to the General describing the movement ; survey of Sugar Mountain and determination to fortify it as it commanded everything at Ticonderoga and Mount Independence ; news of the abandonment of Ticonderoga and Mount Independence by the Americans, who retreat by land towards Castletown, and by water to Skeensborough, leaving cannon, provisions and ammunition behind ; Brigadier Fraser takes possession of the forts, etc., and pursues the rebels ; is joined by Major-General Riedesel , the rebels are attacked and repulsed at Huberton ; mention of the death of Major Grant ; arrival at Skeensborough on the 9th July.

The very great interest of this letter and the fact of some of Burgoyne's correspondence being among Your Lordship's Manuscripts reported on by the Royal Commission make it a pardonable digression to trace here the narrative of this campaign to a little later date.

[Here follow several pages of narration of Burgoyne's campaign.]

No. 12. Various ; as, Stores for Boston in 1775 ; naval statements and other papers relative to the naval enquiry into Lord Sandwich's administration of the Admiralty, 1781–2 ; clipped and deficient money ; excise in Ireland ; linen stamped for sale in Scotland ; some public records left in a Mr. Carrington's custody in 1770, etc.

No. 13. Letters from India and the Cape of Good Hope. Amongst them is an abstract of proceedings relative to Bombay and the Mahrattas dated November and December, 1777. There is also an interesting letter from Mr. Philip Francis (of " Junius " reputation) to George Wombewell, Esq., dated Calcutta, September 19, 1778, enclosing the proposal of a Mr Croftes to Warren Hastings, to pay into the Treasury ten lakhs of Sicca rupees for China Bills on the East India Company This proceeding was strongly objected to by Mr. Francis, as shown in his letter. Accompanying the letter is an account from Colonel Matthew Leslie to Warren Hastings of some fighting at " Camp Rage Gheer." The Chairman and Deputy Chairman of the East India Company write to Mr. Robinson on the 15th December, 1781, transmitting papers from India for the information of Lord North (these should be read with similar papers noted in the Appendix to the Royal Commission Report). From the Cape of Good Hope are two letters written by Richard Lewin to Peter Michell, and dated respectively 30 January and 3 March, 1781. Lewin was appointed to reside at the Cape by the Committee of Fort St. George for the purpose of transmitting intelligence. His letters contain useful information ; the first enclosing a list of ships composing the French Armament which sailed from the French islands for India in October, 1780.

Mr. Robinson's interest in Indian Affairs is very manifest from the quantity of papers relating to the subject in both sections of these manuscripts. [A quotation from Wraxall follows.]

No. 14. Various letters, dated in the years 1800–1802, addressed by Mr. George Atkinson, an intimate friend and fellow-worker of Mr. Robinson, to that gentleman and others, refer to a dispute which arose on the subject of the unsettled accounts depending between the estate of Messrs. Mure and that of the late Mr Richard Atkinson Mr George Atkinson and a Mr. Clayton on their side appear to have been somewhat dilatory in their endeavours to bring matters to an amicable adjustment although professedly desiring to do so ; as George Atkinson, on the 13th January, 1802, states that he doubts the sincerity of the assignees' wishes to this end, in view of the unjustifiable claims in which they persist. Lady Margaret Fordyce appears to have had a claim on the late Richard Atkinson, for amongst the letters is one from her to Mr. Robinson, dated 14 June, 1800, soliciting his services in her behalf To this he kindly replies on the 21st June, telling her he would do what he could.

C. FAMILY PAPERS.

Packets 15 to 18.

No. 15. Five papers with reference to the claims of John, Lord Bergavenny and Lord Maynard to the Office of Chief Larderer at the coronation of Charles II and of James II. Four of these papers are written in French and are interesting from their nature and age.

No 16 An interesting report drawn up by Mr. Robinson dated Wyke House, November 18, 1796, containing correspondence between himself, William Pitt and Lord Abergavenny on the subject of the latter's desire to get a vacant Green Riband from the Government   Mr Pitt, however, gave it to Lord Aylesbury in deference to the Queen's desire.   Mr. Pitt's letters being somewhat rare, we quote one written by him to Mr. Robinson on the 18th July, 1786.

" Dear Sir · It would give me very real pleasure to be instrumental in promoting Lord Abergavenny's Request, and to have an opportunity of shewing my attention to your wishes.   I will certainly not fail to lay his Lordship's Application before the King. At the same time I ought not to conceal from you, that although no absolute decision has yet been made respecting the Green Riband, more than one application has been some days since made to His Majesty, which would render it extremely difficult in the present moment to confer it on Lord Abergavenny, notwithstanding his Rank and Pretensions are undoubtedly entitled to great Consideration.   I am with great Truth, Dear Sir, Your most obedient and faithful Servant, W. Pitt "

Lord Abergavenny threatened, as is shown in this correspondence, to oppose the Government strongly unless the Green Riband was given to him in preference to Lord Aylesbury.   He does not, however, appear to have done so, and, on another vacancy for the Riband, occasioned by Lord Mansfield's death, he wrote again to Mr. Pitt, begging his interest on his behalf.   The correspondence or report (which is 15 pages long) concludes with Mr. Robinson strongly supporting the application.

No. 17. A packet containing   Two letters from Lord Abergavenny in June and July, 1784, on the subject of his son, Lord Nevill, vacating his seat for Seaforth to stand for Monmouthshire ; draft of a letter from Mr. Robinson, 26 January, 1787, to Lord Hawkesbury whose letter is No. 635 in the Appendix already referred to ; a letter from Lord Nevill, 10 September, 1785, announcing the death of his father , subsequent letters to the end of the year on his (Lord Abergavenny's) affairs on his succession to the title

No. 18 Letters from John Robinson to Henry Nevill, who married Robinson's only daughter, Mary.   These extend from 1781 to 1785.   They are of a purely family character and shew the great affection he had for his daughter and other members of his . family.   Those which relate to his daughter's engagement to Lord Nevill give an insight into Mr. Robinson's practical good sense and kindly disposition, as also do others telling of the trouble he took to prepare a suitable house for his daughter and son-in-law. We have also clear evidence of Robinson's love of hospitality in the frequent mention of the company he entertained. It appears, too, that he was fond of hunting and other sport, as several of his letters tell of days spent in the hunting field and the quantity of game bagged by him. The accounts given of visits paid to the houses of several friends shew incidentally how much his company was valued. Altogether, judging from his public services and private correspondence, Mr Robinson was a man of a very gifted mind and of a kindly and generous heart

Having briefly sketched the principal contents of these most valuable manuscripts in Box H it now remains for me to repeat to Your Lordship my warmest thanks for the very great pleasure I have had in perusing them. I especially desire to convey my grateful thanks for the kind permission so readily extended to me to make photographic copies of some of the papers, and I venture to put into the box a copy of each of the Facsimiles so made

INDEX[1]

---

[1] There was not space to make the index comprehensive of all the names and places mentioned in the book. The names included in the index can therefore only be regarded as representing the editor's selection. Names of Parliamentary constituencies and members or candidates mentioned in connection therewith are omitted They will be found in the lists referred to s v. "Memoranda," "Parliament," "Scotland," etc.

Printed in Great Britain by Butler & Tanner, *Frome and London*

Printed in Great Britain
by Amazon.co.uk, Ltd.,
Marston Gate.